Cocktails & Snacks

Cocktails & Snacks

Edited by Helen Chester

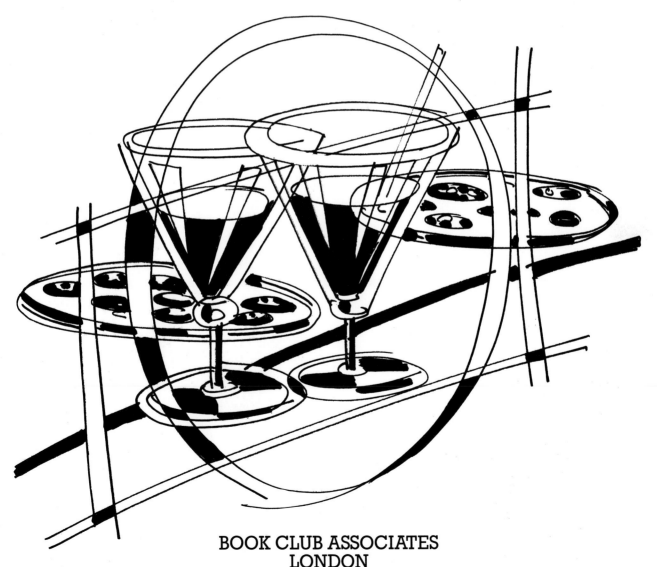

BOOK CLUB ASSOCIATES
LONDON

Acknowledgements

The publishers would like to thank the
following organizations and companies for
their help in contributing material to this
book:

The British Egg Information Service; British
Sausage Bureau; Cheeses from Switzerland
Limited; Dairy Produce Advisory Service of
the Milk Marketing Board; Danish Food
Centre, London; Dutch Dairy Bureau; Flour
Advisory Bureau; The Homepride Kitchen –
Spillers Foods; Lea and Perrins
Worcestershire Sauce; National Dairy
Centre; Sea Fish Kitchen; The Zanzibar

We would also like to thank the following
organizations for kindly supplying
photographs:

The British Egg Information Service (page
89); National Dairy Centre (page 76); Sea
Fish Kitchen (page 69).

Line drawings by Robin Lawrie
Filmset in Rockwell Light by
Filmtype Services Limited,
Scarborough, North Yorkshire.

Printed and bound in Portugal by
Gris Impressores S.R.A.L., Lisbon

Contents

Note

It is important to follow *either* the metric *or* the imperial measures when using this book. Do *not* use a combination of measures.

Cocktails

Basic Equipment

Cocktail shaker – Two principal types are available: a standard shaker and a Boston shaker.

The standard shaker has a base for ingredients, a built-in strainer and a fitted cap. It should never be filled more than four-fifths full. It is generally made of stainless steel.

The Boston shaker, used professionally, is more complicated to handle.

Mixing glass – This is used for stirring cocktails. It should have a lip and be used in conjunction with a bar spoon which resembles a very long teaspoon.

Hawthorn strainer – This is flat with a spring coiled round the edge. It is used mainly to strain stirred cocktails.

Ice bucket and tongs

Ice hammer

Corkscrew and bottle opener

Bitters bottles with nozzles – These enable bitters to be obtained in 'dash' quantities.

Tots, measures, pourers – These are very helpful in measuring correct quantities.

Liquidizer or blender – Not vital but can be very useful.

Sharp knife and a chopping board – For slicing fruits and paring peel.

Straws

Glasses – Stemmed, both small and medium in size
Tumblers and long glasses
Wine goblets

Note Do not over-fill glasses; allow for the inclusion of ice and decoration. Avoid using coloured glass as it will detract from its contents.

Basic Ingredients

Spirits and Liqueurs – Gin, Scotch whisky, vodka, light and dark rum, brandy, Cointreau, tequila.

Wines and fortified wines – Port, sherry, red and white wine, dry, bianco and red vermouth, Campari.

Miscellaneous – Grenadine. Angostura bitters, Tabasco sauce, Worcestershire sauce, oranges, lemons, limes, lime cordial, maraschino cherries, green olives and soda water.

Ice – This is best prepared in a freezer rather than in a domestic refrigerator.

To make cracked ice, use an ice hammer with a pointed head.

To crush ice, put ice blocks in a cloth, and hammer them hard with a mallet or rolling-pin.

To colour ice, add a few drops of edible food colouring before freezing.

Sugar syrup – To make a readily available quantity, boil 450 g/1 lb sugar in 600 ml/1 pint water.

To make enough for individual recipes, boil 15 ml/1 tablespoon sugar in 30 ml/2 tablespoons water.

All cocktails serve 1 person

Brandy and Liqueur-based Cocktails

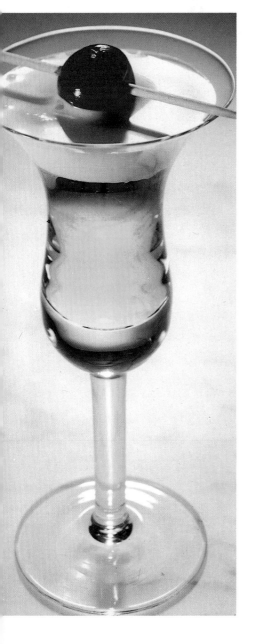

Alexander

2–3 ice cubes
20 ml/¾ fl oz brandy
20 ml/¾ fl oz crème de cacao
20 ml/¾ fl oz cream

Crack ice and put in a shaker with other ingredients. Shake well and strain into a cocktail glass.

Angel's Kiss

40 ml/1½ fl oz apricot brandy
15 ml/½ fl oz cream
1 cocktail cherry

Pour apricot brandy into a pousse-café glass. Add cream, pouring it gently over back of a spoon so that it floats on surface. Spear cherry on a cocktail stick and use to decorate.

Applejack Rabbit

2–3 ice cubes
25 ml/1 fl oz applejack **or** Calvados
20 ml/¾ fl oz orange juice
10 ml/2 teaspoons lemon juice
5 ml/1 teaspoon sugar syrup
1 dash orange bitters

Crack ice and put in a shaker with other ingredients. Shake well and strain into a cocktail glass.

Left: *Angel's Kiss*

Above: *April Shower*

April Shower

2 ice cubes
25 ml/1 fl oz brandy
25 ml/1 fl oz Bénédictine
50 ml/2 fl oz orange juice
soda water

Put ice in a tall goblet with brandy and Bénédictine. Stir well and add orange juice. Top up with soda water and serve with a straw.

Apricot Cooler

3 ice cubes
25 ml/1 fl oz apricot brandy
25 ml/1 fl oz orange juice
25 ml/1 fl oz lemon juice
5 ml/1 teaspoon grenadine
soda water

Put ice in a goblet with apricot brandy, orange juice, lemon juice and grenadine. Stir well and top up with soda water.

Betsy Ross

2–3 ice cubes
25 ml/1 fl oz brandy
25 ml/1 fl oz port
2 dashes Cointreau
1 dash Angostura bitters

Crack ice and put in a shaker with other ingredients. Shake well and strain into a cocktail glass.

Between the Sheets

2–3 ice cubes
20 ml/¾ fl oz brandy
20 ml/¾ fl oz white rum
20 ml/¾ fl oz Cointreau
15 ml/½ fl oz orange juice

Crack ice and put in a shaker with other ingredients. Shake well and strain into a large cocktail glass.

Brandy Cocktail

1–2 ice cubes
40 ml/1½ fl oz brandy
20 ml/¾ fl oz red vermouth
2 dashes Angostura bitters
a piece of lemon peel (optional)

Crack ice and put in a mixing glass. Add brandy, vermouth and bitters. Stir well and strain into a cocktail glass. Add piece of lemon peel, if liked.

Brandy Crusta

15 ml/½ fl oz lemon juice
15 ml/1 tablespoon caster sugar
2–3 ice cubes
50 ml/2 fl oz brandy
5 ml/1 teaspoon sugar syrup
3 dashes maraschino
2 dashes Angostura bitters
a spiral of lemon peel

Dip rim of a large cocktail glass first in lemon juice, shaking off excess, then in sugar. Allow frosting to dry. Crack ice and put in a shaker with brandy, sugar syrup, maraschino and bitters. Shake well and strain into glass. Decorate with spiral of lemon peel.

Brandy Daisy

2–3 ice cubes
25 ml/1 fl oz brandy
15 ml/½ fl oz lemon juice
10 ml/2 teaspoons grenadine
soda water
3–4 cocktail cherries

Crack ice and put in a shaker with brandy, lemon juice and grenadine. Shake well and strain into a champagne glass. Top up with soda water. Decorate with cherries and serve with a cocktail stick.

Brandy Fix

40 ml/1½ fl oz brandy
20 ml/¾ fl oz cherry brandy
15 ml/½ fl oz lemon juice
5 ml/1 teaspoon sugar syrup
1 ice cube
1 lemon slice

Put brandy, cherry brandy, lemon juice and sugar syrup in a small goblet. Stir well. Crush ice and add to glass. Lay lemon slice on top. Serve with a straw.

Brandy Flip

2–3 ice cubes
1 egg yolk
10 ml/2 teaspoons sugar syrup
50 ml/2 fl oz brandy
nutmeg (optional)

Crack ice and put in a shaker with egg yolk, sugar syrup and brandy. Shake very well and strain into a flip glass. Grate a little nutmeg over top, if liked, and serve with a straw.

Brandy Highball

3 ice cubes
25 ml/1 fl oz brandy
5 ml/1 teaspoon lemon juice
5 ml/1 teaspoon sugar syrup
1 dash orange bitters
soda water

Crack one ice cube and put in shaker. Add brandy, lemon juice, sugar syrup and bitters. Shake well and strain into a tumbler. Add remaining ice and top up with soda water.

Brandy Smash

5 ml/1 teaspoon caster sugar
5 ml/1 teaspoon water
3 sprigs of mint
50 ml/2 fl oz brandy
3–4 ice cubes
3–4 lemon, lime **or** orange slices
2 strawberries (optional)
1–2 grapes (optional)

Put sugar in a shaker with water. Add mint, crush well with a spoon and remove. Add brandy and shake well. Crush ice and put in a balloon glass. Strain contents of shaker into glass and decorate with lemon, lime or orange slices and other available fruits. Serve with a straw and spoon.

Calvados Cocktail

2–3 ice cubes
25 ml/1 fl oz Calvados
25 ml/1 fl oz Cointreau
15 ml/½ fl oz orange juice
3 dashes orange bitters

Crack ice and put in a shaker with other ingredients. Shake and strain into a cocktail glass.

Calvados Smash

2–3 ice cubes
30 ml/2 tablespoons mixed fruit
15 ml/1 teaspoon caster sugar
soda water
3 sprigs of mint
25 ml/1 fl oz Calvados
3 dashes crème de menthe
1 dash Bénédictine
apple juice
1 mint leaf

Crush ice, put in a tall glass and add fruit. Put sugar in a shaker and add a shot of soda water. Add sprigs of mint and crush well with a spoon. Add calvados, crème de menthe and Bénédictine, and shake well. Strain into glass and top up with apple juice. Decorate with mint leaf and serve with a straw.

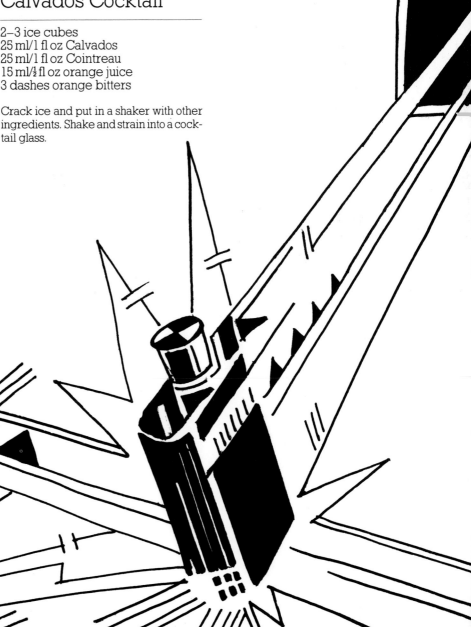

Chartreuse Daisy

2–3 ice cubes
40 ml/1½ fl oz brandy
20 ml/¾ fl oz green Chartreuse
5 ml/1 teaspoon lemon juice
soda water
3 cocktail cherries

Crack ice and put in a shaker with brandy, Chartreuse and lemon juice. Shake and strain into a shallow champagne glass. Top up with soda water and decorate with cherries. Serve with a cocktail stick.

Cherry Blossom

2–3 ice cubes
25 ml/1 fl oz brandy
20 ml/¾ fl oz orange juice
15 ml/½ fl oz cherry brandy
3 dashes Cointreau
3 dashes grenadine
2–5 cocktail cherries

Crack ice and put in a shaker with all other ingredients except cherries. Shake well and strain into a cocktail glass. Decorate with cherries.

Chartreuse Daisy

Chicago Cocktail

2 ice cubes
40 ml/1½ fl oz brandy
5 ml/1 teaspoon Cointreau
1 dash Angostura bitters
sparkling wine

Put ice in a mixing glass with brandy, Cointreau and bitters. Stir well and strain into a shallow champagne glass. Top up with sparkling wine and serve with a straw.

Chocolate Soldier

2 ice cubes
25 ml/1 fl oz brandy
20 ml/¾ fl oz dry vermouth
10 ml/2 teaspoons crème de cacao
1 dash orange bitters

Crack ice and put in an electric blender with other ingredients. Blend and pour into a shallow goblet.

Grasshopper

25 ml/1 fl oz crème de cacao
25 ml/1 fl oz green crème de menthe

Pour crème de cacao into a pousse-café glass. Add crème de menthe, pouring it gently over back of a spoon so that it floats on surface. Serve with a straw.

Island Dream

3–4 ice cubes
10 ml/2 teaspoons Cointreau
10 ml/2 teaspoons grenadine
10 ml/2 teaspoons orange juice
10 ml/2 teaspoons lemon juice
white rum
1 cocktail cherry
1 lemon slice

Crush ice and put in a tumbler with
Cointreau, grenadine, orange juice and
lemon juice. Top up with rum to taste and
stir well. Add cherry and fix lemon slice
on rim of glass. Serve with a straw.

Island Highball

2 ice cubes
15 ml/½ fl oz brandy
15 ml/½ fl oz gin
15 ml/½ fl oz red vermouth
1 dash orange bitters
soda water

Put ice in a tumbler with brandy, gin, vermouth and bitters. Stir and top up to taste
with soda water. Serve with a straw.

Below: *Island Dream, Island Highball*

Honeymoon

2–3 ice cubes
25 ml/1 fl oz Calvados
15 ml/½ fl oz Bénédictine
10 ml/2 teaspoons orange juice
3 dashes Cointreau

Crack ice and put in a shaker with other
ingredients. Shake and strain into a cocktail glass.

Above: *Honeymoon*

International

2–3 ice cubes
20 ml/¾ fl oz brandy
20 ml/¾ fl oz green Chartreuse
15 ml/½ fl oz pineapple juice
1 lemon wedge

Crack ice and put in a shaker with brandy, Chartreuse and pineapple juice. Shake very well and strain into a cocktail glass. Add lemon wedge and serve with a straw.

Kirsch Cobbler

4 ice cubes
40 ml/1½ fl oz kirsch
40 ml/1½ fl oz maraschino
6–8 cocktail cherries
soda water

Crush ice and put in a goblet. Add kirsch, maraschino and cherries. Stir and top up with soda water. Serve with a straw and spoon.

Klondyke Cocktail

3 ice cubes
40 ml/1½ fl oz Calvados
15 ml/½ fl oz dry vermouth
1 dash Angostura bitters
1 olive
a piece of lemon peel

Put ice in a mixing glass with calvados, vermouth and bitters. Stir well and strain into a cocktail glass. Decorate with olive and squeeze lemon peel over top. Serve with a cocktail stick.

Lone Tree Cooler

2–3 ice cubes
40 ml/1½ fl oz apricot brandy
25 ml/1 fl oz lemon juice
20 ml/¾ fl oz lime juice
1 dash grenadine
1 dash Angostura bitters
soda water

Crush ice and put in a shaker with all other ingredients except soda water. Shake and pour into a tall stemmed glass. Top up with soda water and serve with a straw.

Melon Cobbler

4 ice cubes
4–6 balls cantaloupe melon
4–6 balls watermelon
2 dashes brandy
2 dashes Cointreau
champagne

Crush ice and put in a goblet. Add melon, then brandy and Cointreau. Top up with champagne. Serve with a straw and a spoon.

Morning Glory

2–3 ice cubes
20 ml/¾ fl oz brandy
20 ml/¾ fl oz Bourbon whisky
10 ml/2 teaspoons sugar syrup
2 dashes Cointreau
1 dash Pernod
soda water
spiral of lemon peel

Put ice in a mixing glass with brandy, whisky, sugar syrup, Cointreau and Pernod. Stir well and strain into a small tumbler or balloon glass. Top up with soda water, and stir. Decorate with spiral of lemon peel.

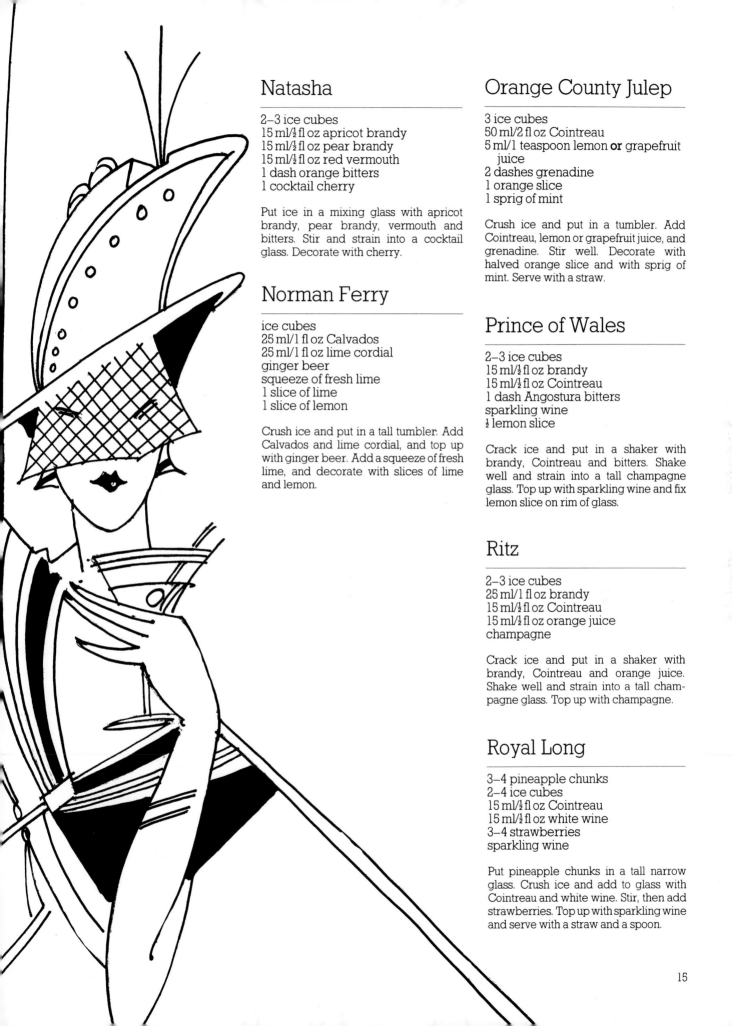

Natasha

2–3 ice cubes
15 ml/½ fl oz apricot brandy
15 ml/½ fl oz pear brandy
15 ml/½ fl oz red vermouth
1 dash orange bitters
1 cocktail cherry

Put ice in a mixing glass with apricot brandy, pear brandy, vermouth and bitters. Stir and strain into a cocktail glass. Decorate with cherry.

Norman Ferry

ice cubes
25 ml/1 fl oz Calvados
25 ml/1 fl oz lime cordial
ginger beer
squeeze of fresh lime
1 slice of lime
1 slice of lemon

Crush ice and put in a tall tumbler. Add Calvados and lime cordial, and top up with ginger beer. Add a squeeze of fresh lime, and decorate with slices of lime and lemon.

Orange County Julep

3 ice cubes
50 ml/2 fl oz Cointreau
5 ml/1 teaspoon lemon **or** grapefruit
    juice
2 dashes grenadine
1 orange slice
1 sprig of mint

Crush ice and put in a tumbler. Add Cointreau, lemon or grapefruit juice, and grenadine. Stir well. Decorate with halved orange slice and with sprig of mint. Serve with a straw.

Prince of Wales

2–3 ice cubes
15 ml/½ fl oz brandy
15 ml/½ fl oz Cointreau
1 dash Angostura bitters
sparkling wine
½ lemon slice

Crack ice and put in a shaker with brandy, Cointreau and bitters. Shake well and strain into a tall champagne glass. Top up with sparkling wine and fix lemon slice on rim of glass.

Ritz

2–3 ice cubes
25 ml/1 fl oz brandy
15 ml/½ fl oz Cointreau
15 ml/½ fl oz orange juice
champagne

Crack ice and put in a shaker with brandy, Cointreau and orange juice. Shake well and strain into a tall champagne glass. Top up with champagne.

Royal Long

3–4 pineapple chunks
2–4 ice cubes
15 ml/½ fl oz Cointreau
15 ml/½ fl oz white wine
3–4 strawberries
sparkling wine

Put pineapple chunks in a tall narrow glass. Crush ice and add to glass with Cointreau and white wine. Stir, then add strawberries. Top up with sparkling wine and serve with a straw and a spoon.

Upton

1 egg yolk
5 ml/1 teaspoon caster sugar
50 ml/2 fl oz brandy

Slide egg yolk into a shallow glass.
Sprinkle with sugar and add brandy.
Do not stir this drink, but swallow it in
one gulp.

Upton

Yellow Parrot

2–3 ice cubes
25 ml/1 fl oz yellow Chartreuse
20 ml/⅔ fl oz gin
20 ml/⅔ fl oz Bénédictine
1 cocktail cherry

Crack ice and put in a shaker with
Chartreuse, gin and Bénédictine.
Shake and strain into a cocktail glass.
Decorate with cherry and serve with a
cocktail stick.

Sidecar

2–3 ice cubes
25 ml/1 fl oz brandy
15 ml/½ fl oz Cointreau
15 ml/½ fl oz lemon juice
1 cocktail cherry

Crack ice and put in a shaker with
brandy, Cointreau and lemon juice.
Shake and strain into a cocktail glass.
Spear cherry on a cocktail stick and use
to decorate.

Stinger

2–3 ice cubes
25 ml/1 fl oz brandy
25 ml/1 fl oz green crème de menthe

Crack ice and put in a shaker with
brandy and crème de menthe. Shake
and strain into a cocktail glass.

Swiss Sunset

2–3 ice cubes
20 ml/⅔ fl oz brandy
20 ml/⅔ fl oz mandarin orange
    liqueur
10 ml/2 teaspoons grapefruit juice
10 ml/2 teaspoons lemon juice

Crack ice and put in a shaker with other
ingredients. Shake and strain into a cocktail glass.

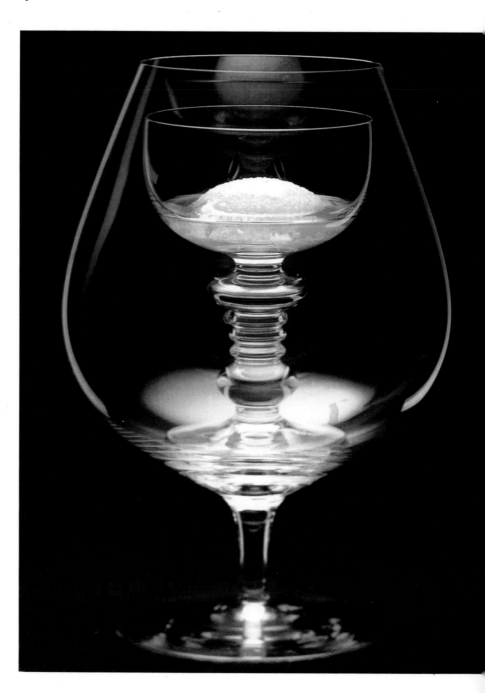

Gin-based Cocktails

Alaska

40 ml/1½ fl oz gin
15 ml/½ fl oz yellow Chartreuse

Put the ingredients in a shaker and shake
well. Strain into a cocktail glass.

Angel's Face

2– fl oz 3 ice cubes
20 ml/¾ fl oz gin
20 ml/¾ fl oz apricot brandy
10 ml/2 teaspoons Calvados

Crack ice and put in a shaker with other
ingredients. Shake well and strain into a
cocktail glass.

Berlin

3 ice cubes
20 ml/¾ fl oz gin
20 ml/¾ fl oz Madeira
20 ml/¾ fl oz orange juice
1 dash Angostura bitters

Crush ice and put in a shaker with other
ingredients. Shake well and pour into a
cocktail glass. Serve with a straw.

Alaska

Bijou

2 ice cubes
15 ml/½ fl oz gin
15 ml/½ fl oz green Chartreuse
15 ml/½ fl oz red vermouth
1 dash orange bitters
1 olive
piece of lemon peel

Put ice in a mixing glass with gin,
Chartreuse, vermouth and bitters. Stir
well and strain into a cocktail glass. Spear
olive on a cocktail stick and use to
decorate. Squeeze lemon peel over top.

Bloodhound

4 ice cubes
15 ml/½ fl oz gin
15 ml/½ fl oz dry vermouth
15 ml/½ fl oz red vermouth
2– fl oz 3 dashes strawberry liqueur
4 strawberries

Crack ice. Put half cracked ice in an
electric blender with gin, vermouths,
strawberry liqueur and two strawberries. Blend briefly and strain into a
cocktail glass. Add remaining cracked
ice and decorate with remaining strawberries. Serve with a straw and a spoon.

Blue Lady

2– fl oz 3 ice cubes
25 ml/1 gin
15 ml/½ fl oz blue curaçao
15 ml/½ fl oz lemon juice
1 cocktail cherry

Crack ice and put in a shaker with gin, curaçao and lemon juice. Shake well and strain into a cocktail glass. Decorate with cherry.

Bronx

2– fl oz 3 ice cubes
15 ml/½ fl oz gin
15 ml/½ fl oz dry vermouth
15 ml/½ fl oz red vermouth
15 ml/½ fl oz orange juice
1 dash Angostura bitters
spiral of orange peel

Crack ice and put in a shaker with gin, vermouths, orange juice and bitters. Shake well and strain into a cocktail glass. Spear orange peel on a cocktail stick and use to decorate.

Charleston

2–3 ice cubes
15 ml/½ fl oz gin
15 ml/½ fl oz dry vermouth
15 ml/½ fl oz bianco vermouth
10 ml/2 teaspoons maraschino
5 ml/1 teaspoon kirsch
5 ml/1 teaspoon Cointreau
piece of lemon peel

Put ice in a mixing glass with gin, vermouths, maraschino, kirsch and Cointreau. Stir well and strain into a cocktail glass. Squeeze lemon peel over top.

Charlie Chaplin

2–3 ice cubes
25 ml/1 fl oz gin
20 ml/¾ fl oz lemon juice
15 ml/½ fl oz apricot brandy
1 cocktail cherry

Crack ice and put in a shaker with gin, lemon juice and apricot brandy. Shake well, strain into a cocktail glass. Decorate with cherry, serve with a cocktail stick.

Clover Club

2–3 ice cubes
1 egg white
15 ml/½ fl oz lemon juice
40 ml/1½ fl oz gin
20 ml/¾ fl oz grenadine

Crack ice and put in a shaker with other ingredients. Shake very well and strain into a small goblet.

Cooperstown

2–3 ice cubes
25 ml/1 fl oz gin
15 ml/½ fl oz dry vermouth
15 ml/½ fl oz bianco vermouth
1 sprig of mint

Put ice in a mixing glass with gin and vermouths. Stir well and strain into a cocktail glass. Decorate with sprig of mint.

Derby

40 ml/1½ fl oz gin
15 ml/½ fl oz peach brandy
1 sprig of mint

Chill gin and peach brandy, then pour into a cocktail glass and stir. Decorate with sprig of mint.

Empire

2–3 ice cubes
25 ml/1 fl oz gin
15 ml/½ fl oz Calvados
15 ml/½ fl oz apricot brandy
2 cocktail cherries

Put ice in a mixing glass with gin, Calvados and apricot brandy. Stir well and strain into a cocktail glass. Decorate with cherries and serve with a cocktail stick.

Eton Blazer

3–4 ice cubes
25 ml/1 fl oz gin
25 ml/1 fl oz kirsch
15 ml/½ fl oz lemon juice
10 ml/2 teaspoons sugar syrup
soda water
2 cocktail cherries

Place ice, gin, kirsch, lemon juice and sugar syrup in a tumbler. Stir, then top up with soda water. Decorate with cherries.

Gimlet

2–3 ice cubes
50 ml/2 fl oz gin
25 ml/1 fl oz lime juice cordial
soda water

Put ice in a mixing glass with gin and lime juice cordial. Stir well and strain into a large cocktail glass. Add a shot of soda water.

Gin Rickey

2–3 ice cubes
50 ml/2 fl oz gin
25 ml/1 fl oz lime **or** lemon juice
1 dash grenadine
soda water
spiral of lime **or** lemon peel

Put ice in a tall glass with gin, lime or lemon juice and grenadine. Stir and top up with soda water. Decorate with spiral of lime or lemon peel.

Gin Sling

2–3 ice cubes
40 ml/1½ fl oz gin
20 ml/¾ fl oz lemon juice
10 ml/2 teaspoons caster sugar
1 dash Angostura bitters
mineral water

Put ice in a tumbler with gin, lemon juice, sugar and bitters. Stir and top up with mineral water.

Gin Fizz

2–3 ice cubes
40 ml/1½ fl oz gin
25 ml/1 fl oz lemon juice
10 ml/2 teaspoons sugar syrup
soda water

Crack ice and put in a shaker with gin,
lemon juice and sugar syrup. Shake very
well and strain into a tall glass. Top up
with soda water to taste and serve with
a straw.

Gin Oyster

5 ml/1 teaspoon gin
1 egg yolk
10 ml/2 teaspoons tomato ketchup
1 dash Worcestershire sauce
1 dash lemon juice
salt and pepper
paprika
nutmeg

Put gin in a shallow glass. Slide in egg
yolk. Add tomato ketchup, Worcestershire sauce and lemon juice. Sprinkle
with salt, pepper and paprika, and grate
over a little nutmeg. Do not stir this drink,
but swallow it in one gulp.

Gin Punch

3 ice cubes
40 ml/1½ fl oz gin
15 ml/½ fl oz lemon juice
10 ml/2 teaspoons caster sugar
2 dashes maraschino
3–4 cocktail cherries
3–4 pineapple chunks

Crush ice and put in a shallow tumbler.
Add gin, lemon juice, sugar and
maraschino. Stir, then decorate with
cherries and pineapple chunks. Serve
with a straw and a spoon.

From left to right: *Gin Punch, Gin
Oyster, Gin Fizz*

John Collins

2–3 ice cubes
25 ml/1 fl oz gin
15 ml/½ fl oz lemon juice
10 ml/2 teaspoons caster sugar
soda water

Put ice in a tumbler with gin, lemon juice and sugar. Top up with soda water, and stir.

Magnolia Blossom

2–3 ice cubes
25 ml/1 fl oz gin
15 ml/½ fl oz cream
10 ml/2 teaspoons lemon juice
2 dashes grenadine

Crack ice and put in a shaker with other ingredients. Shake and strain into a cocktail glass. Serve with a straw.

Golden Fizz

2–3 ice cubes
1 egg yolk
10 ml/2 teaspoons caster sugar
50 ml/2 fl oz gin
25 ml/1 fl oz lemon juice
10 ml/2 teaspoons grenadine
soda water

Crack ice and put in a shaker with egg yolk, sugar, gin, lemon juice and grenadine. Shake very well and strain into a tall tumbler. Top up with soda water and serve with a straw.

Green Hat

2–3 ice cubes
25 ml/1 fl oz gin
25 ml/1 fl oz green crème de menthe
soda water

Put ice in a large goblet or tumbler with gin and crème de menthe. Stir and top up with soda water. Serve with a straw.

Horse's Neck

spiral of lemon peel
ice cubes
50 ml/2 fl oz gin
dry ginger ale

Place one end of lemon peel over edge of a tumbler, allowing remainder to curl inside. Anchor with two ice cubes. Add gin and top up with ginger ale.

Magnolia Blossom

Maiden

2–3 ice cubes
25 ml/1 fl oz orange juice
20 ml/⅔ fl oz gin
20 ml/⅔ fl oz Cointreau
15 ml/½ fl oz lemon juice

Crack ice and put in a shaker with other ingredients. Shake well and strain into a large cocktail glass.

Martini Dry

2–3 ice cubes
50 ml/2 fl oz gin
10 ml/2 teaspoons dry vermouth
piece of lemon peel
1 olive (optional)

Put ice in a mixing glass with gin and vermouth and stir well. Strain into a cocktail glass and squeeze lemon peel over top. If liked, spear olive on a cocktail stick and use to decorate.

Martini Medium

2–3 ice cubes
40 ml/1½ fl oz gin
10 ml/2 teaspoons dry vermouth
10 ml/2 teaspoons red vermouth
piece of orange peel

Put ice in a mixing glass with gin and vermouths. Stir well and strain into a cocktail glass. Decorate with orange peel.

Martini on the Rocks

2–3 ice cubes
50 ml/2 fl oz gin
5 ml/1 teaspoon dry vermouth
1 lemon slice

Put ice in a small tumbler with gin and vermouth. Stir, then decorate with lemon slice.

Martini Sweet

2–3 ice cubes
40 ml/1½ fl oz gin
15 ml/½ fl oz red vermouth
5 ml/1 teaspoon sugar syrup **or** grenadine
1 cocktail cherry

Put ice in a mixing glass with gin, vermouth and sugar syrup or grenadine. Stir well and strain into a cocktail glass. Decorate with cherry and serve with a cocktail stick.

Monte Carlo Imperial

2–3 ice cubes
25 ml/1 fl oz gin
15 ml/½ fl oz white crème de menthe
10 ml/2 teaspoons lime juice
champagne

Crack ice and put in a shaker with gin, crème de menthe and lime juice. Shake and strain into a tall champagne glass. Top up with champagne.

Mule's Hind Leg

2–3 ice cubes
15 ml/½ fl oz gin
15 ml/½ fl oz Calvados
15 ml/½ fl oz Bénédictine
15 ml/½ fl oz apricot brandy
10 ml/2 teaspoons maple syrup

Put ice in a mixing glass with other ingredients. Stir well and strain into a cocktail glass.

Negroni

3 ice cubes
25 ml/1 fl oz gin
15 ml/½ fl oz Campari
15 ml/½ fl oz red vermouth
soda water
1 orange slice

Put ice in a tall tumbler. Add gin, Campari and vermouth, and top up with soda water. Decorate with orange slice and serve with a straw.

Opera

2–3 ice cubes
25 ml/1 fl oz gin
15 ml/½ fl oz Dubonnet
15 ml/½ fl oz maraschino
piece of orange peel

Crack ice and put in a shaker with gin, Dubonnet and maraschino. Shake well and strain into a cocktail glass. Squeeze orange peel over top.

Orange Bloom

2–3 ice cubes
25 ml/1 fl oz gin
15 ml/½ fl oz bianco vermouth
15 ml/½ fl oz Cointreau
1 cocktail cherry

Put ice in a mixing glass with gin, vermouth and Cointreau. Stir well and strain into a cocktail glass. Decorate with cherry.

Peter Pan

2–3 ice cubes
20 ml/¾ fl oz gin
20 ml/¾ fl oz dry vermouth
15 ml/½ fl oz orange juice
10 ml/2 teaspoons peach bitters

Crack ice and put in a shaker with other ingredients. Shake and strain into a cocktail glass.

Pink Gin

3–4 ice cubes
50 ml/2 fl oz gin
3 dashes Angostura bitters

Put ice in a mixing glass with gin and bitters. Stir and strain into a cocktail glass.

From left to right: *Martini on the Rocks*
(page 22), *Martini Sweet* (page 22),
Martini Dry (page 22), *Martini Medium*
(page 22)

Pink Lady Fizz

2–3 ice cubes
1 egg white
10 ml/2 teaspoons grenadine
25 ml/1 fl oz lemon juice
50 ml/2 fl oz gin
soda water

Crack ice and put in a shaker with egg white, grenadine, lemon juice and gin. Shake very well and strain into a goblet. Top up with soda water and serve with a straw.

Pinky

2–3 ice cubes
½ egg white
10 ml/2 teaspoons grenadine
40 ml/1½ fl oz gin

Crack ice and put in a shaker with other ingredients. Shake very well and strain into a cocktail glass.

Queen Elizabeth

2–3 ice cubes
25 ml/1 fl oz gin
15 ml/½ fl oz Cointreau
15 ml/½ fl oz lemon juice
1 dash Pernod
1 cocktail cherry

Crack ice and put in a shaker with gin, Cointreau, lemon juice and Pernod. Shake well and strain into a cocktail glass. Decorate with cherry.

Left: *Pinky and Pink Lady Fizz*

Satan's Whiskers

2–3 ice cubes
15 ml/½ fl oz gin
15 ml/½ fl oz dry vermouth
15 ml/½ fl oz bianco vermouth
15 ml/½ fl oz orange juice
5 ml/1 teaspoon Cointreau
5 ml/1 teaspoon orange bitters

Put ice in a mixing glass with other ingredients. Stir well and strain into a cocktail glass.

Right: *Satan's Whiskers*

Queen's Cocktail

4 pineapple chunks
2–3 ice cubes
25 ml/1 fl oz gin
15 ml/½ fl oz bianco vermouth
15 ml/½ fl oz dry vermouth

Put pineapple chunks in a mixing glass and crush with a spoon. Add other ingredients and stir well. Strain into a cocktail glass.

Queen's Peg

1 large ice cube
25 ml/1 fl oz gin
sparkling wine

Put ice in a goblet, add gin and top up with sparkling wine.

Rose

15 ml/½ fl oz lemon juice
15 ml/1 tablespoon caster sugar
3 ice cubes
25 ml/1 fl oz gin
15 ml/½ fl oz apricot brandy
15 ml/½ fl oz dry vermouth
1 dash grenadine
1 cocktail cherry

Dip rim of a cocktail glass first in lemon juice, shaking off excess, then in sugar. Allow frosting to dry. Put ice in a mixing glass with gin, apricot brandy, vermouth, grenadine and a dash of remaining lemon juice. Stir and strain into cocktail glass. Decorate with cherry.

Ramona Cocktail

1 sprig of mint
2–3 ice cubes
25 ml/1 fl oz gin
25 ml/1 fl oz lemon juice
2 dashes grenadine

Coarsely chop mint. Crack ice and put in a shaker with mint and other ingredients. Shake well and strain into a cocktail glass.

Royal Fizz

2–3 ice cubes
50 ml/2 fl oz orange juice
40 ml/1½ fl oz gin
40 ml/1½ fl oz raspberry brandy
40 ml/1½ fl oz lime juice
soda water

Crack ice and put in a shaker with orange juice, gin, raspberry brandy and lime juice. Shake and strain into a tall tumbler. Top up with soda water and serve with a straw.

Silver Fizz

2–3 ice cubes
1 egg white
5 ml/1 teaspoon caster sugar
25 ml/1 fl oz lemon juice
40 ml/1½ fl oz gin
soda water

Crack ice and put in a shaker with egg white, sugar, lemon juice and gin. Shake very well and strain into a tall tumbler. Top up with soda water, serve with a straw.

Silver Streak

40 ml/1½ fl oz dry gin
25 ml/1 fl oz kümmel
ice cubes

Put ice in a glass and pour gin and kümmel over them.

Singapore Gin Sling

2–3 ice cubes
50 ml/2 fl oz gin
25 ml/1 fl oz lemon juice
15 ml/½ fl oz cherry brandy
15 ml/½ fl oz Cointreau
10 ml/2 teaspoons caster sugar
soda water
1 lemon slice

Put ice in a tall glass with gin, lemon juice, cherry brandy, Cointreau and sugar. Stir and top up with soda water. Decorate with lemon slice.

Tango

2–3 ice cubes
20 ml/¾ fl oz gin
20 ml/¾ fl oz red vermouth
15 ml/½ fl oz Cointreau
15 ml/½ fl oz orange juice
piece of orange peel

Crack ice and put in a shaker with gin, vermouth, Cointreau and orange juice. Shake and strain into a cocktail glass. Squeeze orange peel over top.

Virgin

2 ice cubes
20 ml/¾ fl oz gin
20 ml/¾ fl oz Forbidden Fruit liqueur
10 ml/2 teaspoons crème de menthe

Put ice in a shaker with other ingredients. Shake and pour into a cocktail glass.

White Lady

2–3 ice cubes
½ egg white
10 ml/2 teaspoons lemon juice
25 ml/1 fl oz gin
10 ml/2 teaspoons Cointreau
1 cocktail cherry

Crack ice and put in a shaker with egg white, lemon juice, gin and Cointreau. Shake very well and strain into a cocktail glass. Spear cherry on a cocktail stick and use to decorate.

Yellow Daisy

2–3 ice cubes
40 ml/1½ fl oz gin
40 ml/1½ fl oz dry vermouth
10 ml/2 teaspoons Grand Marnier
1 cocktail cherry

Crack ice and put in a shaker with gin, vermouth and Grand Marnier. Shake well and strain into a large cocktail glass. Decorate with cherry and serve with a cocktail stick.

Rum-based Cocktails

Bacardi Blossom

2–3 ice cubes
40 ml/1½ fl oz Bacardi rum
10 ml/2 teaspoons orange juice
10 ml/2 teaspoons lemon juice
5 ml/1 teaspoon sugar syrup

Crack ice and put in a shaker with other ingredients. Shake well and strain into a cocktail glass.

Bacardi Blossom

Bacardi Highball

3 ice cubes
25 ml/1 fl oz Bacardi rum
25 ml/1 fl oz Cointreau
5 ml/1 teaspoon lemon juice
soda water

Crack two ice cubes and put in a shaker. Add rum, Cointreau and lemon juice. Shake well and strain into a goblet or glass mug. Add remaining ice cube and a shot of soda water. Serve with a straw.

Banana Daiquiri

ice cubes
25 ml/1 fl oz white rum
25 ml/1 fl oz single cream
25 ml/1 fl oz banana liqueur
½ banana

Crush ice and put in a blender with other ingredients. Blend well, then pour into a cocktail glass.

Blue Hawaiian

ice cubes
15 ml/½ fl oz rum
15 ml/½ fl oz blue curaçao
25 ml/1 fl oz single cream
50 ml/2 fl oz coconut cream
100 ml/4 fl oz pineapple juice
1 slice fresh pineapple

Crush ice and put all ingredients, apart from the fresh pineapple, in a blender. Blend well, then pour into a tall tumbler. Decorate with pineapple slice. Spear cherry on a cocktail stick and attach to pineapple.

Cuba Crusta

15 ml/½ fl oz lemon juice
15 ml/1 tablespoon caster sugar
2–3 ice cubes
40 ml/1½ fl oz white rum
10 ml/2 teaspoons pineapple juice
5 ml/1 teaspoon Cointreau
spiral of lemon peel

Dip rim of a goblet first in lemon juice, shaking off excess, then in sugar. Allow frosting to dry. Crack ice and put in a shaker with rum, pineapple juice, Cointreau and remaining lemon juice. Shake and strain into glass. Decorate with spiral of lemon peel.

Left: *Daiquiri American-Style, Daiquiri on the Rocks*

Columbus

2–3 ice cubes
20 ml/¾ fl oz rum
20 ml/¾ fl oz apricot brandy
20 ml/¾ fl oz lime juice

Crack ice and put in a shaker with other ingredients. Shake well and strain into a cocktail glass.

Daiquiri American-style

5–6 ice cubes
50 ml/2 fl oz white rum
25 ml/1 fl oz lime juice
5 ml/1 teaspoon Cointreau
5 ml/1 teaspoon sugar syrup
1 lemon **or** lime slice
1 cocktail cherry

Crack two ice cubes and put in an electric blender with rum, lime juice, Cointreau and sugar syrup. Blend. Crush remaining ice and put in a goblet. Strain contents of blender over crushed ice. Decorate with lemon or lime slice and cherry, and serve with a straw.

Below: *Cuba Libre*

Cuba Libre

2–3 ice cubes
50 ml/2 fl oz white rum
15 ml/½ fl oz lemon juice
Coca-Cola
1 lemon slice

Put ice in a tall tumbler with rum and lemon juice. Top up with Coca-Cola and stir. Fix lemon slice on rim of glass and serve with a straw.

Daiquiri on the Rocks

6–7 ice cubes
50 ml/2 fl oz white rum
25 ml/1 fl oz lime juice
15 ml/½ fl oz sugar syrup

Crack two ice cubes and put in a shaker with rum, lime juice and sugar syrup. Shake very well. Put remaining ice in a tumbler, and strain in contents of shaker. Serve with a straw.

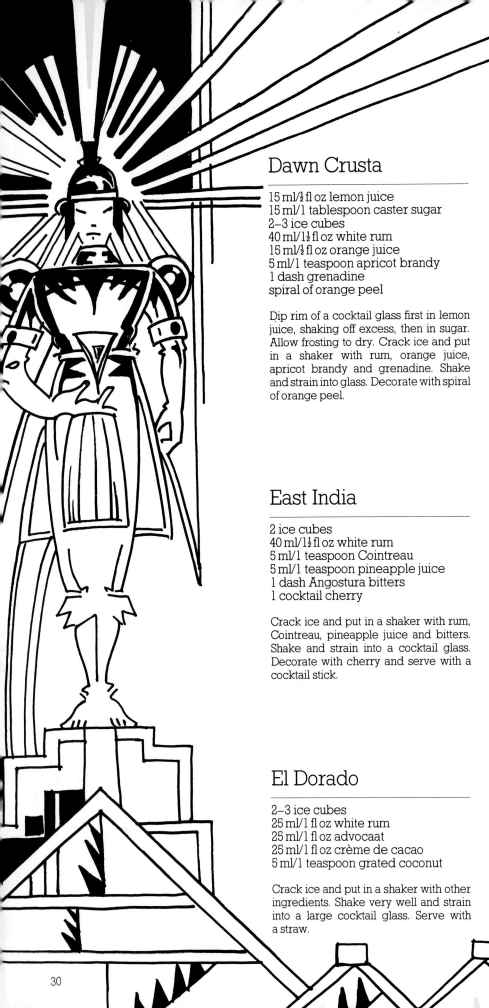

Dawn Crusta

15 ml/½ fl oz lemon juice
15 ml/1 tablespoon caster sugar
2–3 ice cubes
40 ml/1½ fl oz white rum
15 ml/½ fl oz orange juice
5 ml/1 teaspoon apricot brandy
1 dash grenadine
spiral of orange peel

Dip rim of a cocktail glass first in lemon juice, shaking off excess, then in sugar. Allow frosting to dry. Crack ice and put in a shaker with rum, orange juice, apricot brandy and grenadine. Shake and strain into glass. Decorate with spiral of orange peel.

East India

2 ice cubes
40 ml/1½ fl oz white rum
5 ml/1 teaspoon Cointreau
5 ml/1 teaspoon pineapple juice
1 dash Angostura bitters
1 cocktail cherry

Crack ice and put in a shaker with rum, Cointreau, pineapple juice and bitters. Shake and strain into a cocktail glass. Decorate with cherry and serve with a cocktail stick.

El Dorado

2–3 ice cubes
25 ml/1 fl oz white rum
25 ml/1 fl oz advocaat
25 ml/1 fl oz crème de cacao
5 ml/1 teaspoon grated coconut

Crack ice and put in a shaker with other ingredients. Shake very well and strain into a large cocktail glass. Serve with a straw.

Fireman's Sour

2–3 ice cubes
80 ml/3 fl oz white rum
15 ml/½ fl oz lemon juice
5 ml/1 teaspoon grenadine
6 small triangles of lemon
3 cocktail cherries
soda water

Crack ice and put in a shaker with rum, lemon juice and grenadine. Shake well and strain into a tumbler. Decorate with small triangles of lemon and with cherries. Top up with a little soda water.

Good Morning

2–3 ice cubes
1 egg white
5 ml/1 teaspoon sugar syrup
15 ml/½ fl oz lemon juice
20 ml/¾ fl oz rum
20 ml/¾ fl oz port

Crack ice and put in a shaker with other ingredients. Shake very well and strain into a small tumbler. Serve with a straw.

Havana Club

2–3 ice cubes
40 ml/1½ fl oz white rum
20 ml/¾ fl oz red vermouth
1 cocktail cherry

Crack ice and put in a shaker with rum and vermouth. Shake well and strain into a cocktail glass. Spear cherry on a cocktail stick and use to decorate.

Hemingway

2–3 ice cubes
40 ml/1½ fl oz white rum
40 ml/1½ fl oz Cointreau
40 ml/1½ fl oz grapefruit juice
sparkling wine

Crack ice and put in a shaker with rum,
Cointreau and grapefruit juice. Shake
very well and strain into a champagne
glass. Top up with sparkling wine and
serve with a straw.

Horse Guards

2–3 ice cubes
1 egg yolk
20 ml/⅔ fl oz rum
20 ml/⅔ fl oz Cointreau
sparkling wine
spiral of lemon peel

Crack ice and put in a shaker with egg
yolk, rum and Cointreau. Shake very well
and strain into a tumbler. Top up with
sparkling wine and decorate with spiral
of lemon peel. Serve with a straw.

Mai Tai

50 ml/2 fl oz white rum
25 ml/1 fl oz orange juice
25 ml/1 fl oz lime juice
3 ice cubes
3 cocktail cherries
3 pineapple chunks
2 orange slices

Put rum, orange juice and lime juice in a
small goblet and stir well. Crush ice and
add to glass. Decorate with cherries,
pineapple chunks and orange slices.
Serve with a straw and a spoon.

Manhattan Latin

2–3 ice cubes
40 ml/1½ fl oz white rum
20 ml/⅔ fl oz red vermouth

Crush ice and put in a mixing glass with
rum and vermouth. Stir well and pour into
a goblet. Serve with a straw.

Pina Colada

ice cubes
25 ml/1 fl oz white rum
25 ml/1 fl oz single cream
50 ml/2 fl oz coconut cream
100 ml/4 fl oz pineapple juice
1 piece fresh pineapple
1 cocktail cherry

Crush ice and put all ingredients, apart
from pineapple and cherry, in a blender.
Blend well, then pour into a tall tumbler.
Decorate glass with pineapple. Spear
cherry on to a cocktail stick and attach
to pineapple.

Planter's Cocktail

2–3 ice cubes
40 ml/1½ fl oz rum
20 ml/⅔ fl oz orange juice
20 ml/⅔ fl oz lemon juice
2 dashes Angostura bitters
5 ml/1 teaspoon caster sugar
3 pineapple chunks
1 cocktail cherry

Crack ice and put in a shaker with rum,
orange juice, lemon juice, bitters and
sugar. Shake very well and strain into a
large cocktail glass. Decorate with
pineapple chunks and cherry and serve
with a cocktail stick.

Planter's Punch

4–6 ice cubes
50 ml/2 fl oz white rum
15 ml/½ fl oz lemon juice
10 ml/2 teaspoons sugar syrup
1 orange slice
1 cocktail cherry
1 strawberry
2 raspberries

Crack half ice and put in a shaker with rum, lemon juice and sugar syrup. Shake well. Crush remaining ice and put in a tall tumbler. Pour in contents of shaker and stir. Decorate with orange slice, cherry, strawberry and raspberries. Serve with a straw and a spoon.

Presidente

3–4 ice cubes
40 ml/1½ fl oz white rum
25 ml/1 fl oz dry vermouth
spiral of orange peel

Put ice in a mixing glass with rum and vermouth. Stir very well and pour into a small goblet. Decorate with spiral of orange peel.

Quarter Deck

2–3 ice cubes
40 ml/1½ fl oz dark rum
15 ml/½ fl oz sherry
10 ml/2 teaspoons lime juice

Crack ice and put in a shaker with other ingredients. Shake very well and strain into a cocktail glass.

Redskin

2–3 ice cubes
50 ml/2 fl oz white rum
10 ml/2 teaspoons grenadine
pepper
cinnamon
grated nutmeg
1 lemon slice

Crack ice and put in a shaker with rum and grenadine. Add pepper, ground cinnamon and grated nutmeg. Shake and strain into a cocktail glass. Fix lemon slice on rim of glass to decorate.

Above: *Planter's Punch*

Below: *Redskin*

32

Ramona Fizz

2–3 ice cubes
50 ml/2 fl oz white rum
50 ml/2 fl oz lemon juice
25 ml/1 fl oz Cointreau
10 ml/2 teaspoons caster sugar
soda water
1 lemon slice

Crack ice and put in a shaker with rum,
lemon juice, Cointreau and sugar. Shake
very well and strain into a tall tumbler.
Top up with soda water and fix lemon
slice on rim of glass. Serve with a straw.

Royal Bermuda

2–3 ice cubes
40 ml/1½ fl oz white rum
15 ml/½ fl oz lemon juice
5 ml/1 teaspoon Cointreau
5 ml/1 teaspoon sugar syrup

Crack ice and put in a shaker with other
ingredients. Shake and strain into a cocktail glass.

Rocky Mountains Punch

2–3 ice cubes
25 ml/1 fl oz rum
15 ml/½ fl oz lemon juice
10 ml/2 teaspoons maraschino
2–3 pineapple chunks
2–3 strawberries
1–2 cherries
sparkling wine

Crack ice and put in a shaker with rum,
lemon juice and maraschino. Shake and
strain into a goblet. Decorate with fruits
and top up with sparkling wine. Serve
with a straw and a spoon.

Rum Alexander

2–3 ice cubes
25 ml/1 fl oz crème de cacao
15 ml/½ fl oz white rum
15 ml/½ fl oz cream

Crack ice and put in a shaker with other
ingredients. Shake well and strain into a
cocktail glass.

From left to right: *Royal Fizz* (page 26),
Royal Long (page 15), *Royal Bermuda*

Rum Cobbler

3–4 ice cubes
5 ml/1 teaspoon maraschino
5 ml/1 teaspoon grenadine
1 orange slice
1 lime slice
2 cocktail cherries
3–4 pineapple chunks
1–2 strawberries
rum

Crush ice and put in a tall goblet. Add maraschino and grenadine. Decorate with fruits and top up with rum to taste. Serve with a straw and a spoon.

Rum Cocktail

25 ml/1 fl oz white rum
1 dash Angostura bitters
5 ml/1 teaspoon sugar syrup
2 ice cubes
spiral of orange peel
piece of orange peel

Put rum, bitters and sugar syrup in a cocktail glass and stir well. Add ice and decorate with spiral of orange peel. Squeeze remaining piece of orange peel over top.

Rum Flip

2–3 ice cubes
1 egg yolk
10 ml/2 teaspoons sugar syrup
25 ml/1 fl oz rum
25 ml/1 fl oz strong cold tea
10 ml/2 teaspoons Cointreau

Crack ice and put in a shaker with other ingredients. Shake very well and strain into a flip glass. Serve with a straw.

Rum Sour

2–3 ice cubes
40 ml/1½ fl oz white rum
15 ml/½ fl oz lemon juice
5 ml/1 teaspoon sugar syrup
2 cocktail cherries
2 lemon segments
soda water

Crack ice and put in a shaker with rum, lemon juice and sugar syrup. Shake well and strain into a shallow champagne glass. Decorate with cherries and lemon segments and top up with soda water. Serve with a cocktail stick.

Stingray

ice cubes
25 ml/1 fl oz dark rum
4 large fresh strawberries
a dash of fresh lemon juice
a dash of strawberry liqueur **or** syrup

Crush ice and blend with the other ingredients. Pour into a cocktail glass.

Summertime

3 ice cubes
25 ml/1 fl oz rum
25 ml/1 fl oz Cointreau
10 ml/2 teaspoons grenadine
10 ml/2 teaspoons orange juice
10 ml/2 teaspoons lemon juice

Put ice in a mixing glass with other ingredients. Stir well and strain into a large cocktail glass.

Third Rail

2–3 ice cubes
25 ml/1 fl oz rum
10 ml/2 teaspoons dry vermouth
10 ml/2 teaspoons red vermouth
10 ml/2 teaspoons orange juice

Crack ice and put in a shaker with other ingredients. Shake well and strain into a cocktail glass.

Wave of Sylt

15 ml/1 tablespoon caster sugar
50 ml/2 fl oz boiling water
25 ml/1 fl oz rum
25 ml/1 fl oz red wine
1 clove
nutmeg
1 lemon slice

Put sugar in a warmed flameproof punch glass. Add boiling water and stir until sugar has dissolved. Put rum, red wine and clove in a pan, heat until just below boiling point, then pour into glass. Grate a little nutmeg over top and decorate with lemon slice.

XYZ

2–3 ice cubes
25 ml/1 fl oz dark rum
15 ml/½ fl oz Cointreau
15 ml/½ fl oz lemon juice

Crack ice and put in a shaker with other ingredients. Shake and strain into a cocktail glass.

Vodka and Tequila-based Cocktails

Balalaika

2–3 ice cubes
40 ml/1½ fl oz vodka
15 ml/½ fl oz Cointreau
15 ml/½ fl oz lemon juice
spiral of orange peel

Crack ice and put in a shaker with vodka, Cointreau and lemon juice. Shake well and strain into a large cocktail glass. Decorate with spiral of orange peel.

Black Russian

2–3 ice cubes
40 ml/1½ fl oz vodka
15 ml/½ fl oz coffee liqueur

Put ice in a mixing glass with vodka and coffee liqueur. Stir well and pour into a tumbler.

Bloody Mary

25 ml/1 fl oz vodka
50 ml/2 fl oz tomato juice
15 ml/½ fl oz lemon juice
2 dashes Worcestershire sauce
1 ice cube (optional)

Put vodka, tomato juice, lemon juice and Worcestershire sauce in a tumbler and stir. Crush ice, if using, and add to cocktail.

Blue Day

2–3 ice cubes
40 ml/1½ fl oz vodka
20 ml/¾ fl oz blue curaçao
peel ½ lemon
1 lemon slice

Crack ice and put in a shaker with vodka and curaçao. Shake well. Squeeze lemon peel over a cocktail glass. Strain in contents of shaker and fix lemon slice on rim of glass.

Blue Monday Nightcap (1)

2–3 ice cubes
25 ml/1 fl oz vodka
15 ml/½ fl oz blue curaçao
15 ml/½ fl oz Cointreau

Crack ice and put in a shaker with other ingredients. Shake well and strain into a tall glass.

Blue Monday Nightcap (2)

3 ice cubes
40 ml/1½ fl oz vodka
15 ml/½ fl oz Cointreau

Put ice in a mixing glass with vodka and Cointreau. Stir well and pour into a large cocktail glass.

Blue Day

Bullshot

2–3 ice cubes
40 ml/1½ fl oz vodka
50 ml/2 fl oz strong cold beef
   consommé
salt and pepper

Put ice in a mixing glass with other ingredients. Stir and strain into a large cocktail glass.

East Wind

2–3 ice cubes
25 ml/1 fl oz vodka
15 ml/½ fl oz dry vermouth
15 ml/½ fl oz red vermouth
2–3 dashes rum

Crack ice and put in a shaker with other ingredients. Shake and strain into a cocktail glass.

Gipsy

2–3 ice cubes
25 ml/1 fl oz vodka
20 ml/¾ fl oz Bénédictine
1 dash Angostura bitters

Crack ice and put in a shaker with other ingredients. Shake and strain into a cocktail glass.

Green Dragon

2–3 ice cubes
40 ml/1½ fl oz vodka
40 ml/1½ fl oz green crème de
   menthe

Crack ice and put in a shaker with vodka and crème de menthe. Shake and strain into a small goblet.

Above: *Blue Monday Nightcap (1) and (2) (page 36)*   Above: *Gipsy*

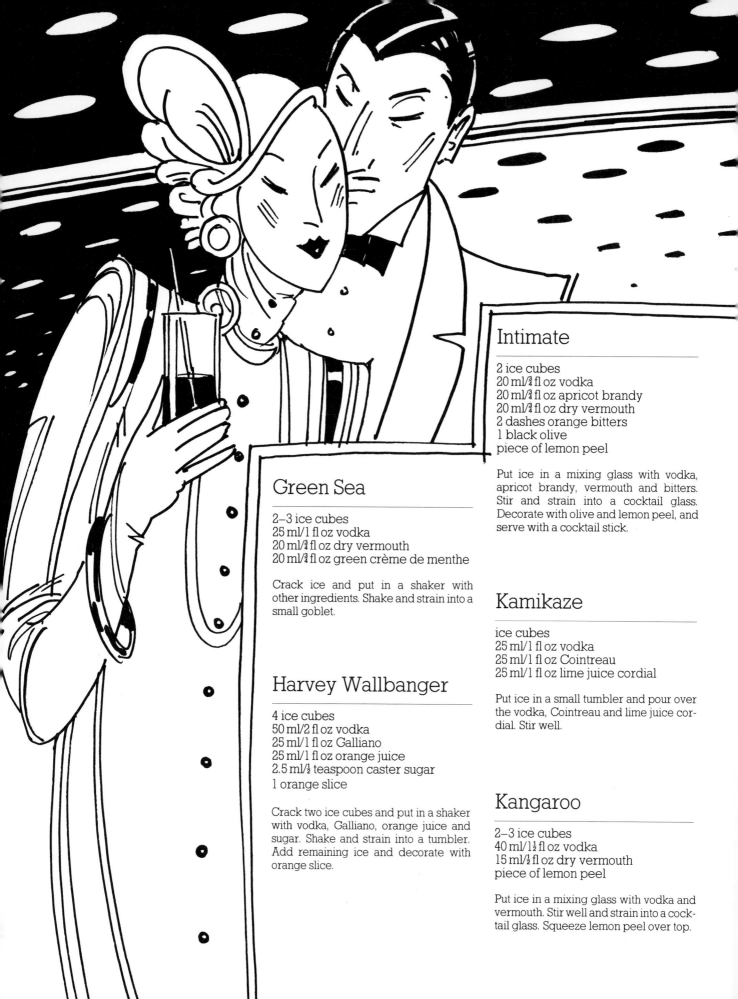

Intimate

2 ice cubes
20 ml/¾ fl oz vodka
20 ml/¾ fl oz apricot brandy
20 ml/¾ fl oz dry vermouth
2 dashes orange bitters
1 black olive
piece of lemon peel

Put ice in a mixing glass with vodka,
apricot brandy, vermouth and bitters.
Stir and strain into a cocktail glass.
Decorate with olive and lemon peel, and
serve with a cocktail stick.

Green Sea

2–3 ice cubes
25 ml/1 fl oz vodka
20 ml/¾ fl oz dry vermouth
20 ml/¾ fl oz green crème de menthe

Crack ice and put in a shaker with
other ingredients. Shake and strain into a
small goblet.

Harvey Wallbanger

4 ice cubes
50 ml/2 fl oz vodka
25 ml/1 fl oz Galliano
25 ml/1 fl oz orange juice
2.5 ml/½ teaspoon caster sugar
1 orange slice

Crack two ice cubes and put in a shaker
with vodka, Galliano, orange juice and
sugar. Shake and strain into a tumbler.
Add remaining ice and decorate with
orange slice.

Kamikaze

ice cubes
25 ml/1 fl oz vodka
25 ml/1 fl oz Cointreau
25 ml/1 fl oz lime juice cordial

Put ice in a small tumbler and pour over
the vodka, Cointreau and lime juice cordial. Stir well.

Kangaroo

2–3 ice cubes
40 ml/1½ fl oz vodka
15 ml/½ fl oz dry vermouth
piece of lemon peel

Put ice in a mixing glass with vodka and
vermouth. Stir well and strain into a cocktail glass. Squeeze lemon peel over top.

Louisa

3 ice cubes, each containing a
    stuffed olive
40 ml/1½ fl oz vodka
65 ml/2½ fl oz tomato juice
5 ml/1 teaspoon lemon juice
4 dashes Worcestershire sauce
salt and pepper
soda water

To prepare frozen stuffed olives, run a
little water into the compartments of an
ice tray, freeze, then add a stuffed olive to
each compartment; fill up with water and
freeze till hard. Place three frozen stuffed
olives in a goblet. Add vodka, tomato
juice, lemon juice, Worcestershire
sauce, salt and pepper. Stir. Top up with
soda water.

Light Blue

ice cubes
25 ml/1 fl oz vodka
15 ml/½ fl oz blue curaçao
15 ml/½ fl oz fresh lemon juice
dash orgeat syrup
1 cocktail cherry
1 lemon slice

Crack ice and put into shaker with vodka,
curaçao, lemon juice and orgeat syrup.
Shake well and strain into a cocktail
glass. Decorate with cherry and a slice of
lemon on a cocktail stick.

Moscow Mule

ice cubes
25 ml/1 fl oz vodka
25 ml/1 fl oz lime cordial
ginger beer
squeeze of fresh lime
1 slice of lemon
1 slice of lime

Put ice into a tall tumbler and pour over
vodka and lime cordial. Top up with
ginger beer, and add a squeeze of
fresh lime. Decorate with slices of lime
and lemon.

Red Tonic

25 ml/1 fl oz vodka
25 ml/1 fl oz grenadine
10 ml/2 teaspoons lemon juice
1 ice cube
1 lemon slice
tonic water

Put vodka, grenadine and lemon juice in
a mixing glass and stir well. Strain into
a tall glass. Add ice and lemon slice
and top up with tonic water. Serve with
a straw.

Screwdriver

2–3 ice cubes
80 ml/3 fl oz orange juice
25 ml/1 fl oz vodka
1 orange slice

Put ice in a mixing glass with orange juice
and vodka. Stir very well and strain into a
tumbler. Fix orange slice on rim of glass
and serve with a straw.

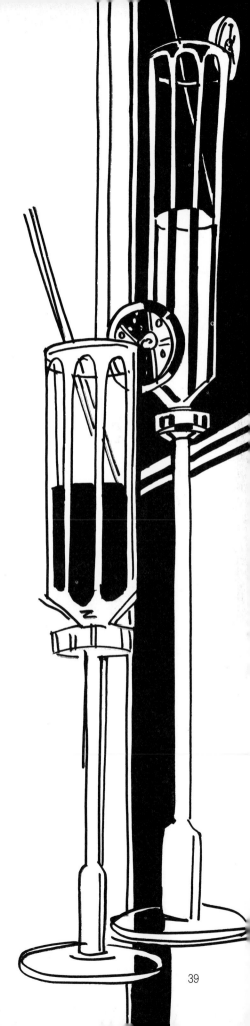

Sputnik (1)

4–6 ice cubes
65 ml/2½ fl oz vodka
25 ml/1 fl oz Fernet Branca
5 ml/1 teaspoon lemon juice
2.5 ml/½ teaspoon caster sugar

Crack half ice and put in a shaker with other ingredients. Shake well and strain into a large cocktail glass. Add remaining ice.

Sputnik (2)

2–3 ice cubes
25 ml/1 fl oz vodka
15 ml/½ fl oz brandy
15 ml/½ fl oz Bourbon whisky
sangrita
Cayenne pepper

Crack ice and put in a shaker with vodka, brandy and whisky. Shake well and strain into a tumbler. Top up with sangrita. Sprinkle with Cayenne pepper and stir well.

Above: *Sputnik (1), Sputnik (2)*

Left: *Tovarich*

Tovarich

8 ice cubes
50 ml/2 fl oz vodka
25 ml/1 fl oz kümmel
20 ml/¾ fl oz lime juice

Crack two ice cubes and put in a shaker with vodka, kümmel and lime juice. Shake well. Crush remaining ice and put in a tall, narrow goblet. Strain in contents of shaker and serve with a straw.

Vodka Fizz

3 ice cubes
50 ml/2 fl oz pineapple juice
40 ml/1½ fl oz vodka
5 ml/1 teaspoon lemon juice
5 ml/1 teaspoon sugar syrup
soda water

Crack two ice cubes and put in a shaker with pineapple juice, vodka, lemon juice and sugar syrup. Shake very well and strain into a tall goblet. Top up with soda water, add remaining ice cube and serve with a straw.

Vodka Gibson

2–3 ice cubes
40 ml/1½ fl oz vodka
15 ml/½ fl oz dry vermouth
2–3 pearl onions

Put ice in a mixing glass with vodka and vermouth. Stir well and strain into a cocktail glass. Decorate with pearl onions and serve with a cocktail stick.

Vodka Gibson, Vodka Fizz

Vodka Crusta

15 ml/½ fl oz orange juice
15 ml/1 tablespoon caster sugar
4–5 ice cubes
40 ml/1½ fl oz vodka
15 ml/½ fl oz brandy
15 ml/½ fl oz red vermouth
1 dash orange bitters
1 dash Angostura bitters
spiral of lemon peel

Dip rim of a goblet first in orange juice, shaking off excess, then in sugar. Allow frosting to dry. Crack ice and put in a shaker with vodka, brandy, vermouth, bitters and two teaspoons of remaining sugar. Shake well and strain into glass. Decorate with spiral of lemon peel.

Vodka Daisy

4–6 pineapple chunks
4–6 ice cubes
50 ml/2 fl oz vodka
10 ml/2 teaspoons sugar syrup
5 ml/1 teaspoon Bénédictine
1 dash maraschino
1 dash Calvados
soda water

Put pineapple chunks in a tall champagne glass. Crack ice and put in a shaker with vodka, sugar syrup, Bénédictine, maraschino and Calvados. Shake very well and strain into glass. Add a shot of soda water and serve with a straw and a spoon.

Vodkatini

ice cubes
50 ml/2 fl oz vodka
10 ml/2 teaspoons dry vermouth
a piece of lemon peel

Put ice in a mixing glass with vodka and vermouth, and stir well. Strain into a cocktail glass and squeeze lemon peel over the top. Decorate with lemon peel.

White Russian

2–3 ice cubes
40 ml/1½ fl oz vodka
15 ml/½ fl oz coffee liqueur
a shot of single cream

Put ice in a shaker with other ingredients and shake well. Pour into a tumbler.

Acapulco

4 ice cubes
50 ml/2 fl oz tequila
25 ml/1 fl oz crème de cassis
5 ml/1 teaspoon sugar syrup
1 lemon slice
soda water

Crush ice and put in a balloon glass. Add tequila, crème de cassis and sugar syrup, and stir well. Add lemon slice and top up with soda water.

Margarita

salt
2–3 ice cubes
25 ml/1 fl oz tequila
15 ml/½ fl oz Cointreau
15 ml/½ fl oz lime **or** lemon juice

Dip rim of a cocktail glass first in water, shaking off excess, then in salt. Allow frosting to dry. Crack ice and put in a shake with other ingredients. Shake and strain into glass.

Tequila Caliente

2–3 ice cubes
40 ml/1½ fl oz tequila
15 ml/½ fl oz crème de cassis
15 ml/½ fl oz lime juice
2 dashes grenadine
soda water

Put ice in a small tumbler with tequila, crème de cassis, lime juice and grenadine. Stir well and add a shot of soda water. Serve with a straw.

Tequila Cocktail

2–3 ice cubes
25 ml/1 fl oz tequila
20 ml/¾ fl oz port
5 ml/1 teaspoon lime juice
2 dashes Angostura bitters

Crack ice and put in a shaker with other ingredients. Shake and strain into a cocktail glass.

Tequila Fix

15 ml/½ fl oz lime juice
10 ml/2 teaspoons honey
50 ml/2 fl oz tequila
2 dashes Cointreau
4–5 ice cubes
1 lemon slice

Put lime juice and honey in a tall tumbler and stir well. Add tequila and Cointreau. Crush ice and add to glass. Stir well and decorate with lemon slice. Serve with a straw.

Tequila Sunrise

6–8 ice cubes
50 ml/2 fl oz tequila
25 ml/1 fl oz grenadine
25 ml/1 fl oz lemon juice
soda water
1 lime slice

Crack half ice and put in a shaker with tequila, grenadine and lemon juice. Shake and strain into a tumbler. Top up with soda water, add remaining ice and fix lime slice on rim of glass. Serve with a straw.

Whisky-based Cocktails

Bourbon Cocktail

2–3 ice cubes
25 ml/1 fl oz Bourbon whisky
10 ml/2 teaspoons Bénédictine
10 ml/2 teaspoons Cointreau
10 ml/2 teaspoons lemon juice
1 dash Angostura bitters

Crack ice and put in a shaker with other ingredients. Shake well and strain into a cocktail glass.

Brooklyn

2–3 ice cubes
25 ml/1 fl oz whisky
25 ml/1 fl oz dry vermouth
10 ml/2 teaspoons maraschino
3 dashes Amer Picon
1 cocktail cherry

Crack ice and put in a shaker with whisky, vermouth, maraschino and Amer Picon. Shake well and strain into a cocktail glass. Decorate with cherry.

Brooklyn

Cape Kennedy

2–3 ice cubes
20 ml/¾ fl oz orange juice
20 ml/¾ fl oz lemon juice
5 ml/1 teaspoon whisky
5 ml/1 teaspoon rum
5 ml/1 teaspoon Bénédictine
5 ml/1 teaspoon sugar syrup

Crack ice and put in a shaker with other
ingredients. Shake well and strain into a
cocktail glass.

Dandy

2–3 ice cubes
20 ml/¾ fl oz Canadian whisky
20 ml/¾ fl oz Cointreau
20 ml/¾ fl oz orange juice

Crack ice and put in a shaker with other
ingredients. Shake well and strain into a
cocktail glass.

Below: *Dandy*

Irish Coffee

10 ml/2 teaspoons caster sugar
40 ml/1½ fl oz Irish whisky
strong hot coffee
15 ml/½ fl oz cream

Put sugar in a goblet and add whisky.
Top up with coffee, and stir. Add cream,
pouring it gently over back of a spoon so
that it floats on surface.

Bourbon Highball

4 ice cubes
25 ml/1 fl oz Bourbon whisky
soda water **or** ginger ale
spiral of lemon peel

Put ice and whisky in a tumbler. Add
soda water or ginger ale to taste.
Decorate with spiral of lemon peel and
serve with a straw.

Below: *Bourbon Highball, Bourbon
Cocktail*

Lieutenant

2–3 ice cubes
25 ml/1 fl oz Bourbon whisky
15 ml/½ fl oz apricot brandy
15 ml/½ fl oz grapefruit juice
5 ml/1 teaspoon sugar syrup
1 cocktail cherry

Crack ice and put in a shaker with
whisky, apricot brandy, grapefruit juice
and sugar syrup. Shake and strain into a
cocktail glass. Decorate with cherry and
serve with a cocktail stick.

Manhattan Dry

2–3 ice cubes
40 ml/1½ fl oz Bourbon whisky
15 ml/½ fl oz dry vermouth
1 dash Angostura bitters

Put ice in a mixing glass with whisky,
vermouth and bitters. Stir well and strain
into a goblet.

Manhattan Sweet

2–3 ice cubes
25 ml/1 fl oz Bourbon whisky
25 ml/1 fl oz bianco vermouth
1 dash Angostura bitters

Put ice in a mixing glass with whisky,
vermouth and bitters. Stir well and strain
into a goblet.

Mary Queen of Scots

15 ml/½ fl oz lemon juice
15 ml/1 tablespoon caster sugar
2–3 ice cubes
25 ml/1 fl oz Scotch whisky
15 ml/½ fl oz Drambuie
15 ml/½ fl oz green Chartreuse
1 cocktail cherry

Dip rim of a cocktail glass first in lemon
juice, shaking off excess, then in sugar.
Allow frosting to dry. Crack ice and put in
a shaker with whisky, Drambuie and
Chartreuse. Shake and strain into glass.
Spear cherry on a cocktail stick and use
to decorate.

Mississippi

2–3 ice cubes
25 ml/1 fl oz rye whisky
25 ml/1 fl oz rum
25 ml/1 fl oz lemon juice
2 dashes sugar syrup
spiral of lemon peel

Crack ice and put in a shaker with
whisky, rum, lemon juice and sugar
syrup. Shake and strain into a small
goblet. To decorate, wind lemon peel
round a wooden skewer or spear it on a
cocktail stick.

Morning Glory Fizz

2–3 ice cubes
1 egg white
10 ml/2 teaspoons caster sugar
25 ml/1 fl oz lemon juice
50 ml/2 fl oz Bourbon whisky
5 ml/1 teaspoon Pernod
soda water

Crush ice and put in a shaker with egg
white, sugar, lemon juice, whisky and
Pernod. Shake very well and strain into a
tumbler or balloon glass. Top up with
soda water and serve with a straw.

Old Pal

2–3 ice cubes
25 ml/1 fl oz Bourbon whisky
15 ml/½ fl oz dry vermouth
15 ml/½ fl oz Campari
piece of lemon peel

Put ice in a mixing glass with whisky, vermouth and Campari. Stir well and strain into a cocktail glass. Add lemon peel.

Rabbit's Revenge

2–3 ice cubes
40 ml/1½ fl oz Bourbon whisky
25 ml/1 fl oz pineapple juice
2–3 dashes grenadine
tonic water
1 orange slice

Put ice in a shaker with whisky, pineapple juice and grenadine. Shake well and pour into a tumbler. Top up with tonic water and fix orange slice on rim of glass. Serve with a straw.

Rickey

1 small lemon
50 ml/2 fl oz whisky
soda water

Cut lemon in two and put in a large tumbler. Press out juice with a spoon and add whisky. Top up with chilled soda water and serve with spoon.

New Yorker

2–3 ice cubes
40 ml/1½ fl oz Bourbon whisky
15 ml/½ fl oz lemon juice
5 ml/1 teaspoon grenadine
piece of orange peel

Crack ice and put in a shaker with whisky, lemon juice and grenadine. Shake and strain into a cocktail glass. Squeeze orange peel over top.

Old-fashioned

5 ml/1 teaspoon caster sugar
5 ml/1 teaspoon water
2 dashes Angostura bitters
2–3 ice cubes
50 ml/2 fl oz Bourbon whisky
1 orange slice
1 cocktail cherry

Put sugar, water and bitters in a small tumbler and stir well. Add ice and whisky. Stir again. Decorate with orange slice and cherry.

Rob Roy

2–3 ice cubes
25 ml/1 fl oz Scotch whisky
25 ml/1 fl oz red vermouth
1 dash Angostura bitters
1 cocktail cherry

Put ice in a mixing glass with whisky, vermouth and bitters. Stir well and strain into a cocktail glass. Decorate with cherry and serve with a cocktail stick.

Rusty Nail

2–3 ice cubes
40 ml/1½ fl oz Scotch whisky
20 ml/¾ fl oz Drambuie
spiral of lemon peel

Put ice in a small tumbler. Add whisky
and Drambuie, and stir. Decorate with
lemon peel.

From left to right: *Manhattan Latin*
(page 31), *Manhattan Cooler* (page 55),
Manhattan Sweet (page 46), *Manhattan
Dry* (page 46)

Stone Fence

2–3 ice cubes
50 ml/2 fl oz whisky
cider
spiral of apple peel

Put ice in a medium-sized tumbler and
add whisky. Top up with cider and
decorate with spiral of apple peel.

Up-to-date

2–3 ice cubes
25 ml/1 fl oz rye whisky
25 ml/1 fl oz sherry
2 dashes Grand Marnier
2 dashes Angostura bitters
piece of lemon peel

Put ice in a mixing glass with whisky,
sherry, Grand Marnier and bitters. Stir
well and strain into a cocktail glass.
Squeeze lemon peel over top.

Wine-based and Non-alcoholic Cocktails

Adonis

3 ice cubes
25 ml/1 fl oz sherry
20 ml/¾ fl oz red vermouth
1 dash Angostura bitters

Put ice in a mixing glass with other ingredients. Stir and strain into a cocktail glass.

Americano

3 ice cubes
25 ml/1 fl oz red vermouth
25 ml/1 fl oz Campari
soda water
piece of lemon rind

Put ice in a tumbler with vermouth and Campari. Stir and top up with soda water. Decorate with piece of lemon rind and serve with a straw.

Americano

American Beauty

50 ml/2 fl oz dry vermouth
50 ml/2 fl oz orange juice
25 ml/1 fl oz brandy
20 ml/¾ fl oz grenadine
4 ice cubes
1 cocktail cherry
2 lemon slices
2 apple **or** orange slices
1 strawberry
5 ml/1 teaspoon port

Put vermouth, orange juice, brandy and grenadine in a mixing glass and stir well. Crush ice and put in a goblet, add contents of mixing glass and decorate with cherry and slices of fruit. Trickle port over top and serve with a straw and a spoon.

American Cooler

3 ice cubes
100 ml/4 fl oz red wine
25 ml/1 fl oz rum
15 ml/½ fl oz sugar syrup
5 ml/1 teaspoon orange juice
5 ml/1 teaspoon lemon juice
soda water
1 lemon slice

Put ice in a tall tumbler with wine, rum, sugar syrup, orange juice and lemon juice. Stir well and top up with soda water. Fix lemon slice on rim of glass.

Amour Crusta

15 ml/½ fl oz lemon juice
15 ml/1 tablespoon caster sugar
2–3 ice cubes
50 ml/2 fl oz tawny port
5 ml/1 teaspoon Cointreau
5 ml/1 teaspoon maraschino
2 dashes peach bitters
2 dashes lime juice
spiral of lemon peel

Dip rim of a cocktail glass first in lemon juice, shaking off excess, then in sugar. Allow frosting to dry. Crack ice and put in a shaker with remaining ingredients except lemon peel. Shake well and strain into glass. Decorate with lemon peel.

Bamboo

2 ice cubes
25 ml/1 fl oz dry vermouth
25 ml/1 fl oz sherry
2 dashes Angostura bitters
1 dash orange bitters
1 cocktail cherry
piece of lemon peel

Put ice, vermouth, sherry, Angostura and orange bitters in a mixing glass. Stir well. Strain into a cocktail glass and decorate with cherry. Squeeze lemon peel over top and serve with a straw.

Beautiful

2–3 ice cubes
15 ml/½ fl oz dry vermouth
10 ml/2 teaspoons white rum
10 ml/2 teaspoons gin
10 ml/2 teaspoons grenadine
10 ml/2 teaspoons orange juice
1 orange slice

Crack ice and put in a shaker with all other ingredients except orange slice. Shake well and strain into a cocktail glass. Fix orange slice on rim of glass.

Buck's Fizz

80 ml/3 fl oz orange juice
champagne

Put orange juice in a tall tumbler and top up with champagne.

Burnt Punch

80 ml/3 fl oz hot water
50 ml/2 fl oz red wine
2 cloves
piece of lemon peel
1 grapefruit slice
3 sugar lumps
15 ml/½ fl oz rum

Put water, wine, cloves and lemon peel in a warmed flameproof punch glass and stir. Lay grapefruit slice on top of glass and place sugar lumps on top. Pour rum over sugar lumps. Stand glass on an asbestos mat and set light to sugar lumps.

Butler's Good Morning Flip

2 ice cubes
1 egg
1 egg yolk
10 ml/2 teaspoons caster sugar
40 ml/1½ fl oz sherry
3 dashes Angostura bitters
sparkling wine

Crush ice and put in a shaker with egg, egg yolk, sugar, sherry and bitters. Shake very well and pour into a large cocktail glass. Top up with sparkling wine and serve with a straw.

Byrrh Cocktail

2–3 ice cubes
20 ml/¾ fl oz Byrrh
20 ml/¾ fl oz rye whisky
20 ml/¾ fl oz red vermouth

Put ice in a mixing glass with other ingredients, and stir. Strain into a cocktail glass.

Campari and Soda

2–3 ice cubes
40 ml/1½ fl oz Campari
soda water
spiral of lemon peel

Put ice in a large tumbler, add Campari and top up with soda water to taste. Decorate with spiral of lemon peel, and serve with a straw.

Campino

15 ml/½ fl oz Campari
15 ml/½ fl oz dry vermouth
15 ml/½ fl oz red vermouth
15 ml/½ fl oz gin
2 dashes crème de cassis
soda water
spiral of orange peel

Put Campari, vermouths, gin and crème de cassis in a mixing glass. Top up with soda water, and stir. Pour into a small tumbler and decorate with spiral of orange peel.

Champagne Cobbler

3–4 ice cubes
3 strawberries (sliced) **or** cocktail cherries
4 peach slices
3 pineapple chunks
5 ml/1 teaspoon Cointreau
5 ml/1 teaspoon maraschino
5 ml/1 teaspoon lemon juice
champagne

Crush ice and put in a goblet. Smooth top of crushed ice and decorate with fruits. Add Cointreau, maraschino and lemon juice and top up with champagne. Serve with a straw and a spoon.

Champagne Cocktail

1 sugar lump
2 dashes Angostura bitters
1 ice cube
15 ml/½ fl oz brandy
champagne
piece of lemon peel

Put sugar lump in a champagne glass and soak with bitters. Add ice and brandy, and top up with champagne. Squeeze lemon peel over top. Serve with a straw.

Champagne Daisy

2–3 ice cubes
20 ml/¾ fl oz yellow Chartreuse
20 ml/¾ fl oz lemon juice
10 ml/2 teaspoons grenadine
champagne
fruit in season

Crack ice and put in a shaker with
Chartreuse, lemon juice and grenadine.
Shake well and strain into a shallow
champagne glass. Top up with cham-
pagne and decorate with pieces of fruit.
Serve with a cocktail stick and a straw.

Champagne Pick-me-up

2–3 ice cubes
15 ml/½ fl oz brandy
15 ml/½ fl oz dry vermouth
5 ml/1 teaspoon sugar syrup
champagne

Put ice in a mixing glass with brandy, vermouth and sugar syrup. Stir and strain
into a goblet. Top up with champagne.

Above: *Creole Punch*

Champagne Flip

2–3 ice cubes
1 egg yolk
10 ml/2 teaspoons sugar syrup
50 ml/2 fl oz Rhine wine
champagne

Crack ice and put in a shaker with egg
yolk, sugar syrup and wine. Shake very
well and strain into a flip glass. Top up
with champagne and serve with a straw.

Opposite: *Champagne Cocktail* (page
51), *Champagne Pick-me-up,*
Champagne Flip

Chicago Cooler

2–3 ice cubes
15 ml/½ fl oz red wine
10 ml/2 teaspoons lemon juice
5 ml/1 teaspoon sugar syrup
ginger ale
1 lemon slice
1 cocktail cherry

Put ice, wine, lemon juice and sugar
syrup in a tumbler, and stir. Top up with
ginger ale. Decorate with lemon slice
and cherry.

Creole Punch

4–6 ice cubes
50 ml/2 fl oz port
15 ml/½ fl oz lemon juice
10 ml/2 teaspoons sugar syrup
5 ml/1 teaspoon brandy
1 lemon slice
1 lime slice
½ orange slice
2 cocktail cherries

Crush ice and put half in a mixing glass
with port, lemon juice, sugar syrup and
brandy. Stir well. Put remaining crushed
ice in a tumbler, strain contents of mixing
glass over it and stir. Decorate with
lemon, lime and orange slices and with
cherries. Serve with a straw.

Chocolate Cocktail

2–3 ice cubes
40 ml/1½ fl oz port
10 ml/2 teaspoons crème de cacao
10 ml/2 teaspoons yellow
 Chartreuse
5 ml/1 teaspoon grated bitter
 chocolate

Crack ice and put in a shaker with other ingredients. Shake well and strain into a cocktail glass.

Continental

2–3 ice cubes
3 dashes dry vermouth
3 dashes red vermouth
2 dashes Cointreau
2 dashes orange bitters
2 dashes maraschino
sparkling wine
1 cocktail cherry

Put ice in a mixing glass with vermouths, Cointreau, bitters and maraschino. Stir well and strain into a shallow champagne glass. Top up with sparkling wine and decorate with cherry.

Crystal Highball

1–2 ice cubes
20 ml/⅔ fl oz bianco vermouth
20 ml/⅔ fl oz red vermouth
20 ml/⅔ fl oz orange juice
soda water
spiral of orange peel

Put ice in a large cocktail glass. Add vermouths and orange juice, and stir. Top up with soda water and decorate with spiral of orange peel. Serve with a straw.

Dubonnet Cocktail

2–3 ice cubes
40 ml/1½ fl oz gin
40 ml/1½ fl oz Dubonnet
piece of lemon peel

Put ice in mixing glass with gin and Dubonnet. Stir and strain into a large cocktail glass. Squeeze lemon peel over top.

Dubonnet Fizz

2–3 ice cubes
40 ml/1½ fl oz Dubonnet
25 ml/1 fl oz orange juice
15 ml/½ fl oz lemon juice
5 ml/1 teaspoon cherry brandy
soda water

Crack ice and put in a shaker with Dubonnet, orange juice, lemon juice and cherry brandy. Shake well and strain into a large cocktail glass. Top up with soda water.

Jeune Homme

2–3 ice cubes
25 ml/1 fl oz dry vermouth
15 ml/½ fl oz gin
15 ml/½ fl oz Cointreau
15 ml/½ fl oz Bénédictine
1 dash Angostura bitters

Crack ice and put in a shaker with other ingredients. Shake and strain into a large cocktail glass.

Kir

15 ml/½ fl oz crème de cassis
dry white wine

Put crème de cassis in wine glass and top
up with wine.

Klondyke Cooler

2–3 ice cubes
25 ml/1 fl oz dry vermouth
25 ml/1 fl oz red vermouth
25 ml/1 fl oz lemon juice
10 ml/2 teaspoons caster sugar
ginger ale

Crack ice and put in a shaker with vermouths, lemon juice and sugar. Shake
very well and strain into a tumbler. Top
up with ginger ale and serve with a straw.

Manhattan Cooler

4 ice cubes
80 ml/3 fl oz claret
15 ml/½ fl oz lemon juice
3 dashes rum
10 ml/2 teaspoons caster sugar
ginger ale
1 cocktail cherry

Crack two ice cubes and put in a shaker
with claret, lemon juice, rum and sugar.
Shake very well and strain into a tall
goblet. Top up to taste with ginger ale.
Add cherry and remaining ice.

Moonlight

3–4 ice cubes
40 ml/1½ fl oz bianco vermouth
15 ml/½ fl oz pear brandy

Put ice in a mixing glass with vermouth
and pear brandy. Stir well and strain into
a cocktail glass.

Myra

2–3 ice cubes
25 ml/1 fl oz red wine
15 ml/½ fl oz vodka
15 ml/½ fl oz dry vermouth

Put ice in a mixing glass with other
ingredients. Stir well and strain into a
cocktail glass.

Pimm's

2–3 ice cubes
40 ml/1½ fl oz Pimm's No 1
2 orange slices
1 lemon slice
lemonade
spiral of cucumber peel **or** sprig of
mint

Put ice in a tall tumbler. Add Pimm's and
orange and lemon slices. Top up with
lemonade and decorate with spiral of
cucumber peel or sprig of mint.

Madeira Cobbler

4 ice cubes
2 peach slices
2 grapes
2 cocktail cherries
3 pineapple chunks
2 teaspoons grenadine
1 dash kirsch
1 dash Cointreau
1 dash maraschino
Madeira

Crush ice and put in a goblet. Add fruits, then grenadine, kirsch, Cointreau and maraschino. Top up with Madeira and serve with a straw and a spoon.

Madeira Flip

2–3 ice cubes
1 egg yolk
10 ml/2 teaspoons sugar syrup
50 ml/2 fl oz Madeira
nutmeg

Crack ice and put in a shaker with egg yolk, sugar syrup and Madeira. Shake well, strain into a tumbler. Grate a little nutmeg over top and serve with a straw.

Port Cobbler

4 ice cubes
65 ml/2½ fl oz port
25 ml/1 fl oz Cointreau
5 ml/1 teaspoon sugar syrup
soda water
5 pineapple chunks
1 cocktail cherry

Crush ice and put in a tall tumbler. Put port, Cointreau and sugar syrup in a shaker and shake well. Pour into tumbler, top up with soda water and decorate with pineapple chunks and cherry. Serve with a straw and a spoon.

Madeira Cobbler, Madeira Flip

Ray Long, Raymond Hitch Cocktail

Ray Long

3 ice cubes
25 ml/1 fl oz bianco vermouth
20 ml/⅔ fl oz brandy
5 ml/1 teaspoon Pernod
1 dash Angostura bitters

Put ice in a mixing glass with other ingredients. Stir well and strain into a cocktail glass.

Red Kiss

2–3 ice cubes
25 ml/1 fl oz dry vermouth
15 ml/½ fl oz gin
15 ml/½ fl oz cherry brandy
spiral of lemon peel

Put ice in a mixing glass with vermouth, gin and cherry brandy. Stir well and strain into a cocktail glass. Decorate with spiral of lemon peel.

Sparkling Grape Cocktail

4 white grapes
3 black grapes
sparkling wine

Spear grapes on wooden cocktail stick and stand stick in a tall champagne glass. Top up with sparkling wine.

Raymond Hitch Cocktail

3 ice cubes
80 ml/3 fl oz bianco vermouth
25 ml/1 fl oz orange juice
1 dash Angostura bitters
1 pineapple slice

Put ice in a mixing glass with vermouth, orange juice and bitters. Stir well and strain into a shallow glass. Decorate with pineapple slice and serve with a spoon.

Sherry Cobbler

4 ice cubes
2 orange slices
1 lemon slice
65 ml/2½ fl oz sherry
15 ml/½ fl oz sugar syrup

Crush ice and put in a tall tumbler or tall champagne glass. Halve orange and lemon slices and add to glass. Pour in sherry and sugar syrup. Stir, and serve with a straw.

Vermouth Addington

2–3 ice cubes
25 ml/1 fl oz dry vermouth
25 ml/1 fl oz bianco vermouth
soda water
spiral of lemon peel

Crack ice and put in a shaker with vermouths. Shake and strain into a goblet. Top up with soda water and decorate with spiral of lemon peel. Serve with a straw.

Vermouth Cassis

2–3 ice cubes
80 ml/3 fl oz dry vermouth
40 ml/1½ fl oz crème de cassis
soda water
piece of lemon peel

Put ice in a goblet with vermouth and crème de cassis. Stir and top up with soda water. Decorate with piece of lemon peel and serve with a straw.

Vermouth Flip

2–3 ice cubes
1 egg yolk
5 ml/1 teaspoon caster sugar
65 ml/2½ fl oz vermouth
nutmeg

Crack ice and put in a shaker with egg yolk, sugar and vermouth. Shake very well and strain into a flip glass. Grate a little nutmeg over top and serve with a straw

Grapefruit Highball

2–3 ice cubes
80 ml/3 fl oz grapefruit juice
25 ml/1 fl oz grenadine
soda water **or** ginger ale

Put ice in a tall tumbler with grapefruit juice and grenadine. Top up with soda water or ginger ale, stir and serve with a straw. This highball may also be served in a hollowed-out grapefruit half.

Orange Cooler

3–4 ice cubes
10 ml/2 teaspoons caster sugar
100 ml/4 fl oz orange juice
ginger ale

Put ice in a large tumbler with sugar and orange juice. Stir and top up with ginger ale. Serve with a straw.

Prairie Oyster

5 ml/1 teaspoon Worcestershire sauce
1 egg yolk
10 ml/2 teaspoons tomato ketchup
2 dashes lemon juice
2 dashes olive oil
salt and pepper
paprika

Put Worcestershire sauce in a shallow glass. Slide in egg yolk. Add tomato ketchup, lemon juice, olive oil, salt, pepper and paprika. Do not stir this drink, but swallow it in one gulp.

Tomato Cocktail

2–3 ice cubes
50 ml/2 fl oz tomato juice
2 dashes lemon juice
1 dash tomato ketchup
1 dash Worcestershire sauce
celery salt

Crack ice and put in a shaker with tomato juice, lemon juice, tomato ketchup, Worcestershire sauce and a little celery salt. Shake well and strain into a small goblet.

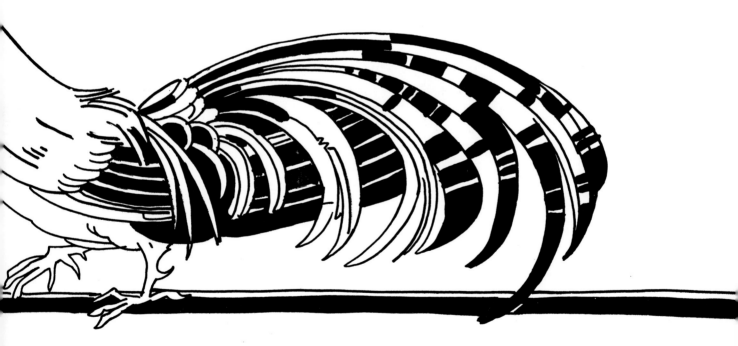

Snacks

Some Points to Note

It is important to bear in mind that snacks are an accompaniment to the cocktails, so that a small selection, hot and cold, plus 1–2 dips are sufficient for a cocktail party.

Serve hot snacks immediately; do not allow them to cool and congeal.

When making toast for canapés, do not prepare it too far in advance as it becomes soft. Remember to drain fried bread well.

Canapés

Three-tier Crackers

200 g/7 oz unsalted butter, softened
2.5 ml/½ teaspoon parsley, chopped
10 ml/1 dessertspoon anchovy paste
5 ml/1 teaspoon mild paprika
salt
75 savoury round crackers

GARNISH
lettuce leaves
25 anchovy fillets, drained
chopped parsley
pearl onions

Cream butter until light and creamy. In one bowl, mix half with parsley and anchovy paste until well blended. Mix remaining butter in another bowl with paprika and salt. Pipe a layer of anchovy butter on to one cracker, gently place a second cracker on top and pipe a layer of the paprika butter on to it. Place a third cracker on top and pipe another layer of the paprika butter on to it. Repeat with the rest of the mixture and crackers.

Arrange the crackers on single lettuce leaves and garnish each with a rolled anchovy fillet, chopped parsley and a pearl onion speared on a cocktail stick.

Three-tier Crackers

Chilli and Pecan Titbits

250 g/9 oz cheese spread
100 g/4 oz cream cheese
150 g/5 oz pecan nuts, chopped
salt
½ chopped onion
pinch of paprika
10 ml/1 dessertspoon lemon juice
small clove of garlic, crushed
    (optional)
45 ml/3 tablespoons mild chilli
    powder
30 savoury round crackers

GARNISH
pecan nuts

Beat cheeses together until well blended. Add nuts, salt and onion, and fold in. Season well with paprika, lemon juice and garlic, if using. Form into a roll 5 cm/2 inches in diameter. Coat with chilli powder and wrap in foil. Chill for 30 minutes or until firm. Remove foil, cut into slices and place each slice on a cracker. Garnish with pecan nuts.

VARIATION
Use walnuts instead of pecan nuts.

Austrian Cheese Savouries

75 g/3 oz cream cheese
50 g/2 oz butter, softened
2.5 ml/½ teaspoon paprika
1.25 ml/¼ teaspoon caraway seeds
5 ml/1 teaspoon capers, finely
    chopped
2.5 ml/½ teaspoon anchovy essence
2.5 ml/½ teaspoon French mustard
10 ml/1 dessertspoon chives **or**
    green part of leek, finely
    chopped
24–30 savoury crackers

GARNISH
whole capers

Beat cream cheese and butter together until smooth and creamy. Stir in paprika, caraway seeds, capers, essence, mustard and chives or leek. Mix well, then pile on to the crackers. Garnish each cracker with a whole caper.

Egg and Olive Crackers

8 hard-boiled eggs
24 savoury round crackers
120 ml/8 tablespoons ham, finely
    chopped
120 ml/8 tablespoons green olives,
    finely chopped
60 ml/4 tablespoons mayonnaise

GARNISH
stuffed green olives

Cut eggs into 1.25 cm/½ inch slices. Remove yolks and place the white rings on the crackers. Mix together yolks, ham, olives and mayonnaise until a paste is formed, then pipe mixture into the cavities of the egg whites. Top each cracker with sliced stuffed olives.

Cucumber and Shrimp Crackers

1 cucumber
cooked shrimps **or** prawns,
    peeled and cleaned
French dressing
savoury round crackers

GARNISH
chopped parsley

Score cucumber with a fork or canelling knife, and cut into thin slices. Marinate shrimps in French dressing for 1 hour, then drain and pat dry. Place a slice of cucumber on a cracker, and top with a shrimp. Garnish with chopped parsley. Repeat with the rest of the ingredients.

Other Toppings for Crackers

HERB MAYONNAISE
Mix chopped parsley and chives with equal quantities of mayonnaise and yoghurt, then add a little dried dill. Garnish with slices of Roquefort or other blue cheese and with sweet peppers marinated in an oil and vinegar dressing.

ANCHOVY MAYONNAISE
Season equal quantities of mayonnaise and yoghurt with anchovy paste, and garnish with anchovy fillets and parsley.

CURRY MAYONNAISE
Mix together equal quantities of mayonnaise and yoghurt plus some hot made mustard. Season with curry powder. Garnish with sliced hard-boiled egg, cheese and lumpfish roe.

SHRIMP TOPPING
Use canned shrimps and mix a little of their liquid with mayonnaise. Season with lemon juice and plenty of mild paprika. Garnish with shrimps and sprigs of fresh dill.

Cheese and Onion Sandwich Croûtes

50 g/2 oz cream cheese
30 ml/2 tablespoons onion, minced
salt and pepper
single **or** double cream (optional)
16 pastry bases, fingers of toast
  or fried bread
paprika

Mix cheese with the onion, and season to taste. Add cream, if necessary, to moisten mixture. Spread on to the canapé bases, and sprinkle with paprika.

Cold Canapé Cocktails

SALAMI AND OLIVES
Place slices of salami on quarters of buttered toast, and garnish with sliced stuffed olives and onion rings.

CAVIAR AND EGG
Put caviar or lumpfish roe on to quarters of buttered toast, and garnish with sliced hard-boiled egg and sprigs of dill.

ASPARAGUS TIPS AND PRAWNS
Arrange asparagus tips, lettuce and prawns on quarters of buttered toast, and garnish with parsley.

CHICKEN AND MANDARIN ORANGES
Arrange slices of chicken breast on quarters of buttered toast, and garnish with mandarin sections, walnut halves and parsley.

STEAK TARTARE AND ANCHOVY FILLETS
Spread steak tartare, seasoned with salt and pepper, on quarters of buttered toast. Garnish with capers and pearl onions, and top with a rolled anchovy fillet.

SMOKED SALMON AND EGG
Arrange slices of smoked salmon on quarters of buttered toast, and garnish with quarters of hard-boiled egg and dill.

TONGUE AND MUSHROOMS
Arrange rolls of cooked tongue on quarters of buttered toast, and garnish with sliced mushrooms and parsley.

ROQUEFORT CREAM
Spread Roquefort cheese mixed with butter on quarters of toast, and garnish with cress and sliced radishes.

Overleaf: *Cold Canapé Cocktails*

Salami Canapés

225 g/8 oz salami
3 hard-boiled eggs
75–90 ml/5–6 tablespoons
   mayonnaise
squares of toast

GARNISH
chopped parsley
pepper strips

Chop salami and eggs finely, and blend with mayonnaise. Spread toast with mixture and sprinkle with chopped parsley. Garnish with strips of pepper.

Cocktail Cheese Savouries

175 g/6 oz plain flour
salt
dry mustard
Cayenne pepper
75 g/3 oz unsalted butter
100 g/4 oz Gouda cheese, grated
1 egg yolk

TOPPINGS
red pepper
green pepper
pieces of lemon rind
pieces of cucumber
anchovy fillets
hard-boiled eggs
gherkins
stuffed olives
slices of cheese

Sift together flour and seasonings into a bowl. Rub in butter until it resembles fine breadcrumbs, then stir in cheese. Add yolk and enough cold water to mix to a firm dough. Roll out on a lightly floured surface to 1.25 cm/½ inch thick, and cut out shapes using 1.25 cm/½ inch diameter cocktail cutters. Place on baking sheets and bake at 200°C/400°F/Gas 6, for 12–15 minutes. Cool on baking sheets.

Using the same cocktail cutters, cut out shapes from the toppings and use to garnish the savouries.

Foie Gras Croûtes

foie gras
double cream
salt and pepper
rounds of fried **or** toasted bread

Pound the foie gras, adding a little cream until consistency is suitable for piping. Rub through a fine sieve, season to taste, and pipe on to bread rounds.

Cream Cheese Starlets

200 g/7 oz cream cheese
30 ml/2 tablespoons milk
salt and pepper
24 small squares of toast, buttered

GARNISH
black grapes
walnut halves

Beat cream cheese with milk to make a soft piping consistency. Season to taste, then pipe mixture on to toast squares, and garnish with grapes or walnut halves.

Chipolata Savouries

PORK CHIPOLATAS AND
ASPARAGUS
Spread rectangles of toast with a savoury butter or mayonnaise, and top with cold chipolatas and asparagus.

DEVILLED PORK CHIPOLATAS
Spread rectangles of toast with butter, and top with stoned prunes, stuffed with an almond, and with cold chipolatas and parsley.

PORK AND TOMATO RELISH
Spread rectangles of toast with a tomato relish, and top with cold chipolatas, tomatoes and lemon wedges.

Gherkin Triangles

triangles of toast
anchovy paste
mayonnaise

GARNISH
chopped egg white
chopped egg yolk
chopped gherkins
stuffed olives

Spread toast with anchovy paste, and moisten edges with mayonnaise. Garnish one edge with finely chopped egg white, the second edge with finely chopped egg yolk, and the third edge with chopped gherkins. Place a stuffed olive in the centre.

Cheese Crisps

4 slices of bread
butter, softened
75 g/3 oz grated cheese
salt and pepper

Spread both sides of bread with butter, and cut into 2.5 cm/1 inch squares. Bake at 160°C/325°F/Gas 3, for 1 hour. Remove from oven and sprinkle liberally with grated cheese. Season to taste and return to oven for another 30 minutes. Serve hot.

Frankfurter and Mustard Bites

4 slices of bread
butter, softened
Dijon mustard
2 frankfurters, sliced diagonally

Spread both sides of bread with butter, and one side with mustard. Cut into 2.5×5 cm/1×2 inch rectangles. Bake, mustard side uppermost, at 160°C/325°F/Gas 3, for 1 hour. Serve garnished with slices of frankfurter.

Ham Wrap-ups

50 g/2 oz butter, softened
5–10 ml/1–2 teaspoons French mustard
18 rectangles of bread, thickly sliced
4 slices of cooked ham (100 g/4 oz)
450 g/1 lb canned sliced peaches, drained
16 maraschino cherries

Mix together butter and mustard, and spread on to bread. Cut each ham slice into quarters, place a peach slice diagonally across each slice of ham, fold over the two opposite corners and secure with a cocktail stick on to the bread. Top with a maraschino cherry.

Ham Rolls

75 ml/5 tablespoons double cream, cottage cheese or curd cheese
30–60 ml/2–4 tablespoons apricot chutney
6 thin slices of cooked ham
small rounds of toast or pumpernickel cocktail rounds

Whip cream lightly, if using; sieve cottage cheese or mash curd cheese. Mix together cream or cheese with chutney. Spread over the ham, and roll up each slice like a Swiss roll. Cut slices into 2.5 cm/1 inch lengths, and place on rounds of toast or pumpernickel.

Pumpernickel and Cheese Cubes

Emmenthal cheese, thinly sliced
pumpernickel slices, buttered

GARNISH
chopped parsley
strips of red pepper

Cut cheese and pimpernickel to the same size. Place one slice of pumpernickel on a board, buttered side up, and cover with a slice of cheese. Cover with a second slice of pumpernickel, buttered side down. Spread the unbuttered side with half the remaining butter. Top with another slice of cheese and another slice of pumpernickel, buttered side down. Spread unbuttered side of this slice with rest of butter. Add the last slice of cheese and the fourth slice of pumpernickel, buttered side down. Wrap in foil and chill for 30 minutes, then cut into cubes with a sharp knife. Garnish with parsley and with pepper strips.

VARIATIONS (fillings)
1) Cream cheese or a creamed mixture of Roquefort or another blue cheese and butter.
2) Cream cheese seasoned partly with grated onion, partly with paprika and salt. Build up the cubes as above, using onion-flavoured cheese for the first and third cheese layers and paprika-flavoured cheese for the middle layer. Chill for 2 hours before cutting into cubes.

Pumpernickel Canapés

225 g/8 oz cooked sausages, finely chopped
15 ml/1 tablespoon horseradish, freshly grated
1 onion, grated
60 ml/4 tablespoons mayonnaise
30 ml/2 tablespoons gherkins, finely chopped
salt and pepper
24 pumpernickel cocktail rounds, buttered

GARNISH
lemon slices **or** fans

Mix together sausages, horseradish, onion, mayonnaise, gherkins and seasoning, and spread on to the pumpernickel rounds. Garnish with lemon slices or fans.

Peppers with Cheese Stuffing

200 g/7 oz cream cheese
75 g/3 oz Roquefort **or** other blue cheese
butter, softened
salt and pepper
1 green and 1 red pepper, deseeded and caps removed
pumpernickel slices, buttered

GARNISH
grapes, halved
stuffed olives, halved

Mix together cream cheese, Roquefort and butter until smooth. Season to taste. Stuff peppers firmly with mixture; do not leave any space. Wrap peppers in foil and chill for 2 hours. Before serving, cut each into twelve slices with a sharp knife. Place on the buttered pumpernickel slices, and garnish with grapes and olives.

Top of page: *Pumpernickel and Cheese Cubes*

Opposite: *Duchy of Cornwall Croûtes*

Party Pinwheels

Cut a sandwich loaf lengthways into about eight slices. Spread each slice with the butter and the filling (see below). Cut off the crusts. Roll each slice up tightly, widthways, like a Swiss roll. Put into a polythene bag or foil, and chill overnight.

Next day, cut each roll into about ten thin rounds.

FILLINGS
1) 100 g/4 oz butter blended with mixed fresh herbs, and topped with 225 g/8 oz thinly sliced tongue.
2) 100 g/4 oz butter, beaten together with 100 g/4 oz grated Danish blue or Stilton cheese and 15 ml/1 tablespoon orange juice.

Duchy of Cornwall Croûtes

175 g/6 oz smoked cod's roe, skinned
freshly ground black pepper
30 ml/2 tablespoons parsley, chopped
1 clove garlic, crushed
150 ml/¼ pint oil
30 ml/2 tablespoons lemon juice
225 g/8 oz hot smoked mackerel, skinned and boned
225 g/8 oz open mushrooms, cleaned and stalked
croûtes of hot toast, buttered

Place roe, pepper, parsley and garlic in a bowl, and mix well. Gradually beat in half the oil to make a good emulsion; stabilize by adding lemon juice and some boiling water. Continue in this way with the rest of the oil. Mash the mackerel, and blend with roe mixture. Fill cavities of mushrooms with the pâté, and garnish with the stalks. Serve on croûtes of hot buttered toast.

Anchovy Croûtes

2 hard-boiled eggs
2.5 ml/½ teaspoon curry paste
   or 5 ml/1 teaspoon curry powder
100 g/4 oz butter, softened
24 rounds or triangles of toast
24 anchovy fillets
paprika
few drops lemon juice

GARNISH
chopped parsley

Separate egg yolks from whites and chop whites finely. Rub yolks through a sieve, and combine with curry paste or powder, and the butter. Mix to a soft paste, and spread toast with mixture. Arrange an anchovy fillet on each piece of toast, and season with paprika. Add a few drops of lemon juice. Heat at 220°C/425°F/Gas 7, for 3–4 minutes. Garnish with chopped egg white and parsley just before serving.

Sardine and Cheese Fingers

8 slices toast
40 ml/4 dessertspoons tomato
 ketchup
450 g/1 lb sardines in tomato
 sauce
225 g/8 oz Cheddar cheese, grated

GARNISH
parsley sprigs

Spread toast with tomato ketchup, and lay sardines evenly on top. Sprinkle with the cheese and cut into fingers. Grill under a slow heat for about 5 minutes or until cheese melts. Serve hot, garnished with parsley.

Hot Savoury Toasts

fingers of toast
any firm non-greasy meat paste
 or liver pâté **or** mashed sardines,
 seasoned with salt, pepper and a
 little tomato paste

Spread toast with one of the mixtures, place on an ovenproof platter, and cover securely with foil. Heat through at 180°C/350°F/Gas 4, for a few minutes until hot.

Devilled Smoked Salmon Croûtes

6–8 slices of toast, buttered
salt and pepper
300 g/11 oz smoked salmon
 trimmings, finely chopped
butter, softened
pinch of curry powder
lemon juice

GARNISH
sprigs of parsley

Sprinkle toast with pepper and a little salt. Pound salmon trimmings thoroughly to make a fairly smooth mixture which can be spread evenly. Mix butter with a pinch of curry powder, a few drops of lemon juice and salt and pepper. Spread pounded salmon on to toast, and coat with curry butter. Cut each slice into three fingers. Heat at 200°C/400°F/Gas 6, for 4–5 minutes. Garnish with parsley, and serve hot.

Angels on Horseback

16 large shelled oysters
16 rashers streaky bacon,
 without rinds
16 fingers of hot toast, buttered

GARNISH
watercress leaves

Wrap each oyster in a bacon rasher. Fasten the rolls with small poultry skewers, and grill for 4–6 minutes, or bake for 10 minutes at 220°C/400°F/Gas 6. Remove the skewers when the 'angels' are cooked, and serve on the toast fingers. Garnish with watercress.

Bacon Olives

250 g/9 oz cooked ham **or** tongue,
   finely chopped
25 g/1 oz breadcrumbs
5 ml/1 teaspoon onion, finely
   chopped
5 ml/1 teaspoon parsley,
   finely chopped
pinch of dried mixed herbs
pinch of grated nutmeg
salt and pepper
2 eggs, beaten
16 thin rashers streaky bacon,
   without rinds
16 rounds of toast **or** pastry canapés

Mix together ham or tongue, breadcrumbs, onion, parsley and herbs, and
add a pinch of nutmeg. Season to taste.
Stir in as much egg as is needed to bind
the mixture. Leave for 30 minutes. Divide
mixture into sixteen portions. Form each
portion into a cork shape, roll in a rasher
of bacon, and secure with string or small
skewers. Bake at 190°C/375°F/Gas ·5,
for about 30 minutes. Serve on toast or
pastry canapés.

Ham Croûtes

butter
40 ml/4 dessertspoons shallot
   or onion, chopped
300 g/11 oz cooked ham, finely
   chopped
4 egg yolks
pepper
16 round slices of fried bread
   or toast

GARNISH
chopped parsley

Melt butter and fry the shallot or onion
until lightly browned. Add ham, and stir
until hot. Add yolks, and season with
pepper. Stir until mixture thickens, then
spoon it on to the bread rounds, and
serve sprinkled with parsley.

Cheese and Sausage Canapés

24 small squares of toast, buttered
French mustard
6 cooked sausages, thinly sliced
100 g/4 oz cheese, finely grated

Spread toast squares with a thin layer
of mustard. Top each with a few slices
of sausage, and sprinkle with
grated cheese. Brown under a grill, and
serve hot.

Scotch Woodcock

40 g/1½ oz butter
6 eggs
45 ml/3 tablespoons milk
salt and pepper
16 quarters of toast, buttered

GARNISH
anchovy fillets
capers

Melt butter in a pan. Beat eggs, milk, and
seasoning together lightly. Pour into the
pan, reduce the heat, and cook gently,
stirring all the time, until just set and
creamy. Divide between the toast and
garnish with small pieces of anchovy
fillet and capers.

71

Pastry-based Snacks and Biscuits

Gruyère Twists

Gruyère Twists

300 g/11 oz prepared puff pastry
75 g/3 oz Gruyère cheese, grated
egg yolk and milk, beaten

Cut pastry in half. Sprinkle 40 g/1½ oz grated cheese over one half, put the other half on top and sprinkle remaining cheese over it. Roll out to 5 mm/¼ inch thick, and cut pastry into strips 7.5 cm/3 inches wide. Pile four strips at a time on top of each other. Glaze with beaten yolk and milk. Cut strips into slices 5 mm/¼ inch thick, and twist into bow shapes. Place on baking sheets and bake at 220°C/425°F/Gas 7, for 10 minutes. Cool on baking sheets.

Paprika and Cheese Sticks

300 g/11 oz prepared puff pastry
75 g/3 oz butter
100 g/4 oz Emmenthal cheese,
  grated
20 ml/4 teaspoons concentrated
  tomato purée
5 ml/1 teaspoon paprika
2 egg yolks, beaten

Roll out pastry on a lightly floured surface into a rectangle 5 mm/¼ inch thick.
  Cream butter until soft and white, then mix with cheese and tomato purée, and season with paprika. Spread this filling over half the pastry, and fold the other half over it. Cut into strips 10 cm/4 inches long and 2.5 cm/1 inch wide, and place on baking sheets. Glaze with beaten egg yolk. Bake at 220°C/425°F/Gas 7, for 15 minutes. Cool on a wire rack. Serve hot or cold.

Salted Caraway Sticks

300 g/11 oz prepared puff pastry
egg yolk and milk, beaten

DECORATION
coarse salt
caraway seeds

Roll out pastry on a lightly floured surface and cut into strips 10 cm/4 inches long and 1.25 cm/½ inch wide. Twist strips, holding each end, to form spiral shapes. Place on baking sheets and sprinkle with salt and caraway seeds. Glaze with beaten yolk and milk. Bake at 220°C/425°F/Gas 7, for 15 minutes. Cool on baking sheets.

Poppyseed Savouries

300 g/11 oz prepared puff pastry
beaten egg yolk
20 stuffed olives, drained
60 g/2½ oz Emmenthal cheese,
    grated

DECORATION
75 g/3 oz poppyseeds

Roll out pastry on a lightly floured surface into a rectangle 30×40 cm/12×16 inches. Cut into forty small rectangles measuring 5×6 cm/2×2½ inches.

Glaze half the rectangles with egg yolk, put a drained olive on each, and sprinkle the centres with a little grated cheese. Put the remaining rectangles on top, and press edges well together with a fork. Glaze lids with egg yolk and sprinkle with poppyseeds. Place on baking sheets. Allow to rest for 15 minutes, then bake at 200°C/400°F/Gas 6 for 10–15 minutes. Serve hot or cold.

Savoury Puff Pastries

300 g/11 oz prepared puff pastry
beaten egg yolk

DECORATION
poppyseeds
caraway seeds
whole almonds
flaked almonds

Roll out pastry on a lightly floured surface, cut into circles and squares, and form looped and spiral shapes. Glaze well with egg yolk. Sprinkle with poppyseeds or caraway seeds, or decorate with whole almonds. Roll spirals in flaked almonds. Place on baking sheets and bake at 220°C/425°F/Gas 7, for 10–15 minutes. Cool on baking sheets.

Poppyseed Savouries

Stilton Whirls

100 g/4 oz Blue Stilton
50 g/2 oz cream cheese
5 ml/1 teaspoon Worcestershire
    sauce
pinch of Cayenne pepper
100 g/4 oz prepared puff pastry

Crumble Stilton into a bowl, mix to a paste with cream cheese, and stir in Worcestershire sauce and Cayenne pepper. Roll out pastry on a lightly floured surface into a rectangle 28×15 cm/11×6 inches, and spread with cheese mixture. Roll up as for a Swiss roll, and chill until firm. Cut into 5 mm/¼ inch slices and put on to baking sheets. Bake at 220°C/425°F/Gas 7, for 15 minutes or until golden-brown. Cool on a wire rack.

Cocktail Sausage Rolls

200 g/7 oz prepared puff pastry
8 sausages **or** 200 g/7 oz sausage-
    meat
beaten egg yolk

Roll out pastry on a lightly floured surface into one thin long rectangle or strip. Skin sausages, if required. Form sausage-meat into two long rolls the same length as strip. Place on pastry, well apart. Cut pastry into two equal strips, each wide enough to wrap round a roll of meat. Dampen one edge of each strip, fold over and press damp and dry edge of each strip together, forming two long rolls. Cut into short lengths, and make diagonal slits in top of each roll. Put on to baking sheets, and glaze with egg yolk. Bake at 230°C/450°F/Gas 8, for 5–7 minutes. Reduce heat to 180°C/350°F/Gas 4, and bake for 15–20 minutes, covering if necessary. Serve hot or cold.

Cheese and Grape Puffs

675 g/1½ lb strong plain flour
salt
250 g/9 oz butter **or** margarine
250 g/9 oz lard
400 ml/¾ pint iced water
egg and water, beaten

FILLING
675 g/1½ lb cream cheese
30 ml/2 tablespoons milk
rind of 1½ small lemons,
    grated
paprika
salt and pepper
175 g/6 oz white grapes,
    halved and stoned
175 g/6 oz black grapes,
    halved and stoned

DECORATION
black and white grapes,
    halved and stoned

Sift together flour and salt into a bowl. Cut fat into walnut-sized pieces and add to flour. Add water, and mix to a firm dough, keeping pieces of fat whole. Use a round-bladed knife. Turn on to a lightly floured surface and knead gently. Roll out to two rectangles each 12.5×30 cm/5×12 inches. Fold into three and press edges firmly to seal. Turn at right angles and roll out once more. Fold and wrap in polythene or foil and chill for 15 minutes. Repeat rolling, folding and resting process twice more. Roll out into two rectangles, each 20×25 cm/8×10 inches. Cut into strips 2.5×25 cm/1×10 inches. Brush one edge of each strip with beaten egg and water, and wind pastry round two-thirds of the length of a cornet mould, beginning at the tip and overlapping slightly. Place well apart on baking trays, and chill for 30 minutes. Brush with beaten egg and water, and bake at 220°C/425°F/Gas 7, for 15–20 minutes. Remove moulds and cool horns on a wire rack.

To make filling, cream together cheese and milk. Beat in lemon rind, paprika and seasoning to taste. Add grapes, and mix well. Place 15 ml/1 tablespoon of mixture in centre of each pastry horn, and decorate with black and white grape halves. Chill before serving.

Devilled Cheese Tarts

350 g/12 oz plain flour
2.5 ml/½ teaspoon salt
Cayenne pepper
175 g/6 oz butter
175 g/6 oz Lancashire cheese
2 eggs, beaten
30–60 ml/2–4 tablespoons cold
    water

FILLING
225 g/8 oz butter, softened
350 g/12 oz Lancashire cheese,
    grated
10 ml/1 dessertspoon curry powder
    or to taste
2 small cooking apples,
    peeled and grated
50 g/2 oz salted peanuts, chopped

GARNISH
chopped chives

Sift flour, salt and Cayenne pepper into a bowl, and rub in fat until mixture resembles fine breadcrumbs. Stir in cheese, eggs and enough cold water to form a stiff dough. Roll out on a lightly floured surface, and cut out shapes to line twenty small oval or round tins. Bake blind at 200°C/400°F/Gas 6, for 15 minutes, then bake for another 10 minutes until cooked. Remove from tins and cool on a wire rack.

To make filling, beat together all ingredients until well mixed, and use to fill pastry cases. Garnish with chives.

Mackerel Barquettes

100 g/4 oz plain flour
salt
Cayenne pepper
50 g/2 oz butter
50 g/2 oz Cheddar cheese, finely
    grated
1 egg yolk
milk

FILLING
175 g/6 oz hot smoked mackerel
    fillet, skinned and boned
75 g/3 oz butter, softened
15 ml/1 tablespoon lemon juice
small clove of garlic, crushed
salt and freshly ground pepper

GARNISH
parsley sprigs

Sift flour, salt and Cayenne pepper into a
bowl, and rub in fat until mixture resembles fine breadcrumbs. Stir in cheese,
egg yolk and enough milk to form a stiff
dough. Roll out on a lightly floured surface to 5 mm/¼ inch thick, and use to line
twelve to eighteen barquette moulds or
patty tins. Bake at 200°C/400°F/Gas 6, for
10 minutes until golden-brown. Cool on a
wire rack.
    To make filling, pound fish with butter
until smooth. Add lemon juice and garlic,
and mix well. Season to taste. Spoon
carefully into pastry cases, and garnish
with parsley.

VARIATIONS
1) Use cooked kipper fillets instead of
   mackerel.
2) Use cooked smoked haddock or cod
   instead of mackerel.

Anchovy Tartlets

75 g/3 oz butter **or** margarine
175 g/6 oz plain flour, sifted
2 egg yolks
few drops of anchovy essence
100 g/4 oz anchovy fillets, drained
2 hard-boiled egg yolks
50 g/2 oz butter, softened
pinch of Cayenne pepper
90 ml/6 tablespoons double cream
few drops of cochineal

GARNISH
paprika
capers

Rub fat into flour, add yolks, anchovy
essence and enough water to mix to a soft
dough. Roll out thinly on a lightly floured
surface, and use to line twenty-four very
small patty tins. Prick bases all over, then
bake at 200°C/400°F/Gas 6, until crisp.
Cool on a wire rack.
    Pound anchovies with hard-boiled
egg yolk and butter until smooth. Season
with a little Cayenne pepper. Whip
cream until fairly stiff, and fold in. Add
colouring, drop by drop, until mixture is
pale pink. Use to fill pastry cases, piling
mixture high in centre. Sprinkle with
paprika, and garnish with capers.

Cheese Straws

100 g/4 oz plain flour
pinch of dry mustard
pinch of salt
pinch of Cayenne pepper
75 g/3 oz butter, softened
75 g/3 oz Parmesan cheese, grated
1 egg yolk

Sift together flour and seasonings into a
bowl. Cream butter until soft and white,
and add flour, cheese, yolk and enough
cold water to form a stiff dough. Roll out
on a lightly floured surface to 5 mm/¼ inch
thick, and cut into fingers about 10 ×
1.25 cm/4 × ½ inch. Place on a baking
sheet and bake at 200°C/400°F/Gas 6, for
8–10 minutes or until lightly browned and
crisp. Cool on baking sheet.

Salty Straws

250 g/9 oz plain flour
pinch of baking powder
pinch of salt
75 ml/5 tablespoons milk
125 g/5 oz butter **or** margarine
egg yolk and milk, beaten

DECORATION
coarse salt

Sift together flour, baking powder and
salt into a bowl. Make a well in the centre,
then add milk and the fat cut up into small
pieces. Knead well until a firm dough is
formed, then chill for 30 minutes. Form
into 10 cm/4 inch strips, and twist,
holding each end, to form a spiral shape. Put on to
a baking sheet and glaze with beaten
egg yolk and milk. Sprinkle with coarse
salt. Bake at 200°C/400°F/Gas 6, for 15
minutes, until crisp. Cool on a wire rack.

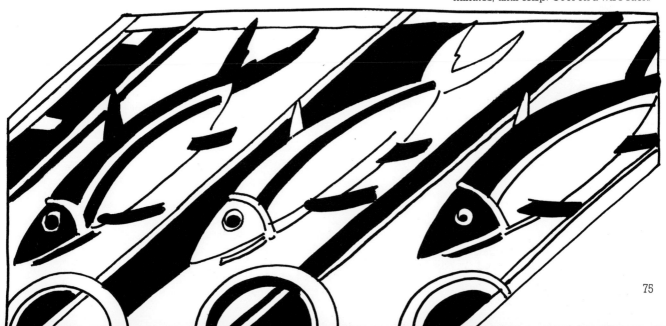

Moreish Straws

100 g/4 oz plain flour
salt
Cayenne pepper
75 g/3 oz butter
50 g/2 oz mature English Cheddar
    cheese, finely grated
1 egg yolk
yeast extract

Sift together flour, salt and Cayenne pepper into a bowl. Rub in butter until mixture resembles fine breadcrumbs, then stir in cheese. Add yolk and enough water to mix to a firm dough. Chill for 30 minutes. Cut dough in half and roll each half into a square approximately 5 mm/¼ inch thick. Spread thin layer of yeast extract over one half and lay other half on top. Roll out again to 5 mm/¼ inch thick. Cut strips 7.5 cm/3 inches long and 5 ml/¼ inch wide, and rings 4 cm/1½ inches in diameter. Twist strips, holding each end, to form a spiral shape. Lay straws and rings on baking sheet, and bake at 200°C/400°F/Gas 6, for 10–15 minutes or until light golden-brown. Cool on baking sheet.

Deep-Fried Cheese Puffs

75 g/3 oz butter
250 ml/8 fl oz water
salt
200 g/7 oz plain flour, sifted
4 eggs, lightly beaten
150 g/5 oz Emmenthal cheese,
    grated
50 g/2 oz flaked almonds
oil for deep frying

Put butter, water and salt in a pan and bring to boil. Remove from heat and beat in flour, all at once, using a wooden spoon. Return to heat and beat well until mixture leaves sides of pan and forms a soft ball. Put into a bowl, cool slightly and beat in eggs, one by one. Add the grated cheese, and mix well. Form pastry into walnut-sized balls, and toss in flaked almonds. Fry three or four at a time at 180°C/350°F, for 4 minutes or until golden-brown. Drain, and serve hot.

Cocktail Choux Buns

50 g/2 oz unsalted butter
150 ml/¼ pint water
65 g/2½ oz plain flour, sifted
2 eggs, lightly beaten

FILLING
25 g/1 oz unsalted butter
25 g/1 oz plain flour
300 ml/½ pint milk
salt and pepper
100 g/4 oz Gouda cheese, grated
50 g/2 oz mushrooms, finely
    chopped
100 g/4 oz cooked ham, finely
    chopped

To make choux pastry, put butter and water in a pan and bring to boil. Remove from heat and beat in flour, all at once, using a wooden spoon. Return to heat and beat well until mixture leaves sides of pan and forms a soft ball. Put into a bowl, cool slightly and beat in eggs, one by one. Put mixture in a piping bag with a 1.25 cm/½ inch nozzle and pipe into very small balls on a greased baking sheet. Bake at 220°C/425°F/Gas 7, for about 10 minutes, then remove from oven and reduce heat to 180°C/350°F/Gas 4. Make a slit in each bun to allow steam to escape. Return to oven for another 10 minutes to allow buns to dry out. Cool on a wire rack.

To make filling, put butter, flour and milk in a pan, and heat, stirring all the time, until sauce boils and thickens. Season to taste, and remove from heat. Stir in cheese, mushrooms and ham. Fill each bun with 5 ml/1 teaspoon of mixture, and serve hot or cold.

Left: *Deep-fried Cheese puffs*

Opposite: *Savoury Bites* (page 83),
Moreish Straws, Stilton Whirls (page 74)

Cheese and Walnut Choux Puffs

100 g/4 oz unsalted butter
300 ml/½ pint water
125 g/5 oz plain flour, sifted
large pinch of salt
4 eggs, lightly beaten

FILLING
225 g/8 oz soft cream cheese
30 ml/2 tablespoons mayonnaise
30 ml/2 tablespoons walnuts,
    chopped
3 gherkins, chopped
salt and pepper

GARNISH
30 ml/2 tablespoons parsley,
    freshly chopped

To make choux puffs, put butter and water in a pan and bring to boil. Remove from heat and beat in flour, all at once, using a wooden spoon. Add salt. Return to heat, and beat well until mixture leaves sides of pan and forms a soft ball. Put into a bowl, cool slightly and beat in eggs, one by one. Continue beating until mixture is smooth and shiny. Spoon teaspoons of mixture on to greased baking sheets. Bake at 220°C/425°F/Gas 7, for 15–20 minutes, then remove from oven and reduce heat to 180°C/350°F/Gas 4. Make a slit in each bun to allow steam to escape. Return to oven for another 10 minutes to allow buns to dry out. Cool on a wire rack.

To make filling, mix cheese and mayonnaise in a bowl. Beat in walnuts, gherkins and seasoning. Fill buns with mixture, and arrange in a pyramid on a serving dish. Sprinkle with parsley.

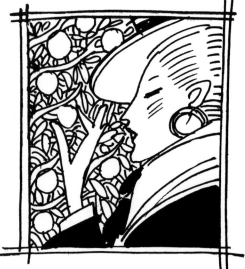

Olive Savouries

250 g/9 oz Cheddar cheese, grated
125 g/5 oz butter
175 g/6 oz plain flour, sifted
pinch of salt
paprika
400 g/14 oz stuffed green olives,
    drained

Put cheese, butter, flour and seasoning in a bowl, and knead to a soft dough. Press an olive into middle of 5 ml/1 teaspoon of dough and shape into a ball. Make sure it is well covered. Put olive savouries on baking sheets, and bake at 230°C/450°F/Gas 8, for about 15 minutes. Serve cold.

Vol-au-vent Bouchées

1 kg/2¼ lb prepared puff pastry
beaten egg

Roll out pastry about 1.25 cm/½ inch thick. Cut into round shapes with a 7.5 cm/3 inch cutter, and place on baking sheets. Glaze with beaten egg. With a smaller cutter, make a circular cut in each case, to form an inner ring, cutting through about half the depth of pastry. Bake at 220°C/425°F/Gas 7, until golden-brown and crisp. When baked, remove inner lid, and scoop out soft inside while still warm. Fill with one of the hot fillings below. Serve immediately.

FILLINGS
1) Mix 500 ml/16 fl oz white sauce with 225 g/8 oz chopped cooked mushrooms, 225 g/8 oz chopped cooked chicken, 10 ml/2 teaspoons lemon juice, and salt and pepper to taste. Heat throroughly.
2) Mix 500 ml/16 fl oz white sauce with 225 g/8 oz cooked flaked haddock, 225 g/8 oz prawns, 30 ml/2 tablespoons sherry, 10 ml/2 teaspoons very finely chopped onion, and salt and pepper to taste. Heat thoroughly.

Cheese Bouchées

175 g/6 oz mushrooms, cleaned
    and stalked
500 g/18 oz bacon, without rinds
3 small onions
75 g/3 oz butter
75 g/3 oz breadcrumbs
45 ml/3 tablespoons tomato ketchup
salt and black pepper
1.25 kg/2 lb 10 oz prepared puff
    pastry
675 g/1½ lb Emmenthal cheese in
    one piece
oil

Mince mushrooms, bacon and onion, and fry in butter for 5 minutes. Add breadcrumbs, tomato ketchup and seasoning to taste. Roll out pastry into three 10 cm/4 inch squares, then cut each into sixteen 2.5 cm/1 inch squares. Slice the cheese into twenty-four squares about 1.25 cm/½ inch in size and 5 mm/¼ inch thick. Place a cheese square on each pastry square, then place an equal quantity of mushroom mixture on each square of cheese.

Moisten the edges of the pastry, place an uncovered square on each filled square, and seal edges well. Fry bouchées at 190°C/375°F for about 10 minutes or until golden. Drain, and serve hot.

Individual Pizzas

150 g/5 oz butter
350 g/12 oz plain flour, sifted
300 ml/½ pint milk
2 onions, chopped
225 g/8 oz streaky bacon, chopped
6 tomatoes, skinned and chopped
30 ml/2 tablespoons concentrated
    tomato purée
2.5 ml/½ teaspoon dried oregano
    or dried mixed herbs
salt and pepper
350 g/12 oz Lancashire cheese

GARNISH
tomato slices
anchovy fillets
olives

Rub 75 g/3 oz butter into flour until mixture resembles fine breadcrumbs. Mix in
milk until mixture forms a stiff dough. Roll
out on a lightly floured surface to 5 mm/
¼ inch thick. Cut into twenty rounds about
7.5 cm/3 inches in diameter, and place on
baking trays.

Melt remaining butter in a pan and add
onion and bacon. Cook gently for 3–4
minutes, then stir in tomatoes, tomato
purée, herbs and seasoning to taste.
Cook for 3 minutes, then spoon on to the
pizza bases. Cover with the cheese and
bake at 200°C/400°F/Gas 6, for 30
minutes. Garnish with slices of tomato,
anchovies and olives.

Devilled Cheese Savouries

450 g/1 lb plain flour
5 ml/1 teaspoon salt
Cayenne pepper
175 g/6 oz butter **or** margarine
60 ml/4 tablespoons water

FILLING
25 g/1 oz butter
25 g/1 oz plain flour
300 ml/½ pint **plus** 90 ml/
    6 tablespoons milk
100 g/4 oz cheese, grated
dried mustard
Cayenne pepper
salt and pepper
50 g/2 oz anchovy fillets, drained

GARNISH
paprika
sprigs of watercress

Sift together flour, salt and Cayenne
pepper into a bowl. Rub in fat until mixture resembles fine breadcrumbs. Add
water and mix to a firm dough. Knead
lightly on a floured surface. Roll out on a
lightly floured surface and use to line
twenty to twenty-four small fluted tartlet
tins. Prick base of each one, and bake
blind at 200°C/400°F/Gas 6, for 10–15
minutes, then remove from tins and cool
on a wire rack.

To make filling, melt butter in pan, add
flour, stir well and cook for 1 minute.
Gradually blend in milk. Bring to boil,
and remove from heat. Add all but 30 ml/
2 tablespoons of cheese, the mustard,
Cayenne pepper and seasoning. Stir
well. Place an anchovy fillet in base
of each pastry case, and pour sauce on
top. Sprinkle remaining cheese and
a pinch of paprika on to top of each
one. Bake at 200°C/400°F/Gas 6, for
10 minutes. Remove from oven and
serve hot, sprinkled with paprika and
garnished with watercress.

Herb Biscuits

200 g/7 oz plain flour
5 ml/1 teaspoon baking powder
pinch of salt
45 ml/3 tablespoons oil
60 ml/4 tablespoons water
30 ml/2 tablespoons herbs,
    freshly chopped (parsley,
    chives, cress, borage, dill)

Sift together flour, baking powder and
salt into a bowl. Make a well in the centre,
then add oil, water and herbs. Knead
well until a smooth dough is formed. Roll
out on a lightly floured surface to 2.5 cm/
1 inch thick, and cut out 5 cm/2 inch round
biscuits. Place on a baking sheet, and
bake at 200°C/400°F/Gas 6, for 15
minutes. Serve warm.

Camembert Biscuits

125 g/5 oz ripe Camembert cheese
75 g/3 oz butter, softened
250 g/9 oz plain flour
10 ml/2 teaspoons baking powder
1 egg
pinch of nutmeg
15 ml/1 tablespoon whisky
beaten egg yolk

DECORATION
hazelnuts
walnuts
cashew nuts
almonds

Carefully remove rind of Camembert.
Mash cheese with fork, then beat in
butter. Sift flour and baking powder into
a bowl. Make a well in the centre, and
add egg. Divide cheese and butter mixture into small pieces and add to flour.
Add nutmeg and whisky to egg in centre.
Working from outside, knead together
until a dough is formed. Chill for 30
minutes. Roll out on a lightly floured surface to 5 mm/¼ inch thick. Cut into small
squares, and place on a baking sheet.
Glaze with egg yolk, and decorate with
nuts. Bake at 200°C/400°F/Gas 6, for 15
minutes, then cool on a wire rack.

French Cheese Biscuits

75 g/3 oz Roquefort cheese
50 g/2 oz butter **or** margarine
5 ml/1 teaspoon single cream
15 ml/1 tablespoon brandy
100 g/4 oz self-raising flour, sifted
pinch of salt
pinch of black pepper
beaten egg yolk

DECORATION (optional)
paprika
grated cheese
caraway seeds
chopped walnuts

Mash cheese with fork, add other ingredients, one by one, apart from egg yolk, and mix to form a smooth dough. Cover, and chill for 30 minutes. Roll out very thinly on a lightly floured surface, and cut out 5 cm/2 inch biscuits. Place on baking sheets, and glaze with egg yolk. Sprinkle, if liked, with one of the decorations. Bake at 180°C/350°F/Gas 4, for 10 minutes. Cool on a wire rack.

Emmenthal Biscuits

250 g/9 oz plain flour, sifted
200 g/7 oz butter
1 egg
200 g/7 oz Emmenthal cheese, grated
beaten egg yolk

DECORATION
poppyseeds
caraway seeds
salt crystals

Place flour in a bowl, make a well in the centre, then add the butter cut up into small pieces. Place egg and cheese in the hollow, and mix together all ingredients. Knead until a smooth dough is formed, then chill for 30 minutes. Roll out on a lightly floured surface, and, using a pastry wheel, cut into 2.5 cm/1 inch diamond shapes and strips 5 cm/2 inches long and 1.25 cm/½ inch wide. Place on baking sheets, and glaze with egg yolk. Sprinkle with poppyseeds, caraway seeds or salt crystals. Bake at 200°C/400°F/Gas 6, for 10 minutes, until crisp, then cool on a wire rack.

Emmenthal Biscuits

Other Snacks

Camembert Cubes

Camembert cheese
breadcrumbs
savoury stick biscuits
butter

GARNISH
lettuce leaves
halved stuffed olives

Cut Camembert into wedges, and toss in breadcrumbs. Shortly before serving, dip savoury biscuits in butter, and stick one in each wedge. Arrange wedges on lettuce leaves and garnish with sliced stuffed olives.

Creamy Coconut Dates

175 g/6 oz cream cheese
30 ml/2 tablespoons double cream
450 g/1 lb dates, stoned
1 egg white, beaten
50 g/2 oz desiccated coconut

Beat together cheese and cream until soft and smooth. Fill dates with mixture, then coat in egg white and coconut. Chill for at least 1 hour before serving, speared on cocktail sticks.

Camembert Cubes

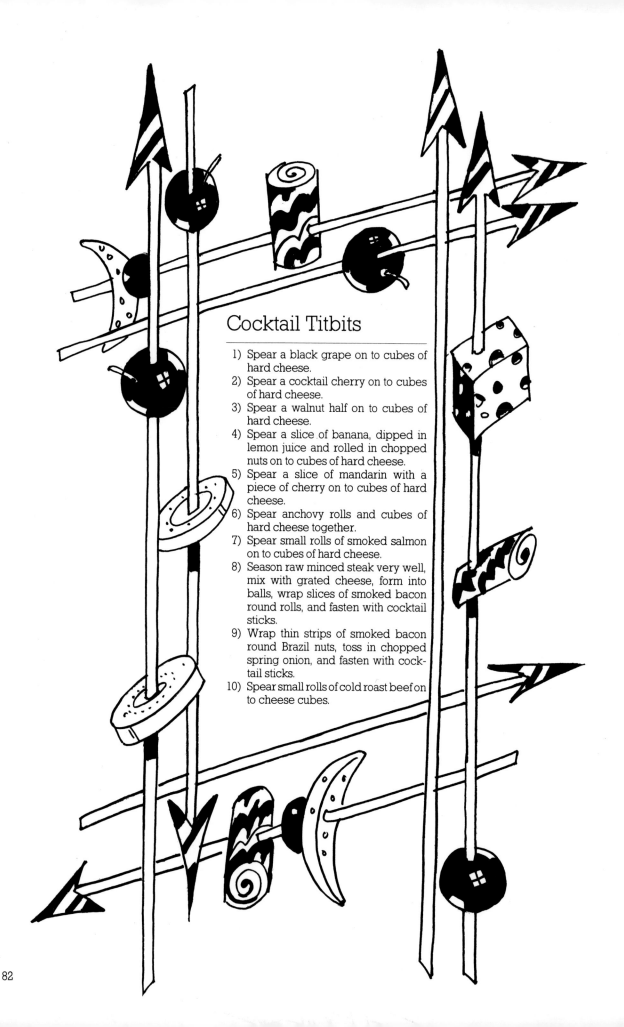

Cocktail Titbits

1) Spear a black grape on to cubes of hard cheese.
2) Spear a cocktail cherry on to cubes of hard cheese.
3) Spear a walnut half on to cubes of hard cheese.
4) Spear a slice of banana, dipped in lemon juice and rolled in chopped nuts on to cubes of hard cheese.
5) Spear a slice of mandarin with a piece of cherry on to cubes of hard cheese.
6) Spear anchovy rolls and cubes of hard cheese together.
7) Spear small rolls of smoked salmon on to cubes of hard cheese.
8) Season raw minced steak very well, mix with grated cheese, form into balls, wrap slices of smoked bacon round rolls, and fasten with cocktail sticks.
9) Wrap thin strips of smoked bacon round Brazil nuts, toss in chopped spring onion, and fasten with cocktail sticks.
10) Spear small rolls of cold roast beef on to cheese cubes.

Cocktail Cheese Balls

225 g/8 oz Edam cheese, grated
50 g/2 oz unsalted butter
7.5 ml/½ tablespoon made mustard
22.5–30 ml/1½–2 tablespoons double
    cream
salt and pepper

DECORATION
ham, finely chopped
fresh parsley, finely chopped
mixed nuts, finely chopped

Mix together all ingredients until soft,
then form into small balls about 2.5 cm/
1 inch in size. Roll in either finely
chopped ham, parsley or nuts, and serve
skewered by cocktail sticks.

Savoury Bites

75 g/3 oz cream cheese
100 g/4 oz mature Cheddar cheese,
    finely grated
10 pearl onions, finely chopped
25 g/1 oz gherkins, finely chopped
salt
Cayenne pepper
2 drops of Tabasco sauce

DECORATION
digestive biscuits, crushed
nuts, finely chopped

Mix together cream cheese and grated
cheese to form a smooth paste. Add
onions and gherkins, stir in salt, Cayenne
pepper and Tabasco sauce to taste, and
mix well. Form into small balls, and chill.
Just before serving, roll balls in biscuit
crumbs or chopped nuts.

Salami and Cheese Cubes

cream cheese
salt and pepper
Cayenne pepper **or** mustard
thin slices of salami

Soften cheese, and season well with salt,
pepper and Cayenne pepper or mustard. Sandwich between slices of salami,
building them up until they are 2.5 cm/
1 inch high. Chill to firm up. Cut into
cubes, and spear on to cocktail sticks.

Cheese and Ham Cornets

450 g/1 lb cream cheese
100 g/4 oz walnuts, chopped
120 ml/8 tablespoons parsley **or**
    chives, chopped
60 ml/4 tablespoons mayonnaise
salt and freshly ground black
    pepper
20 slices cooked ham

GARNISH
watercress

Beat cream cheese until soft and smooth.
Mix in walnuts, parsley or chives, and
mayonnaise. Season to taste. Form each
slice of ham into a cornet shape and
secure with a wooden cocktail stick.
Divide cream cheese mixture between
cornets, and arrange on a plate of
watercress.

Stuffed Mushrooms

125 g/5 oz sardines, drained
30 ml/2 tablespoons double cream
100 g/4 oz Cheddar cheese, grated
50 g/2 oz onion, chopped
45 ml/3 tablespoons mayonnaise
salt
Cayenne pepper
15 ml/1 tablespoon parsley,
    chopped
12 button mushrooms, cleaned and
    stalked

GARNISH
parsley sprigs

Mash sardines with fork. Whip cream
until stiff, and mix together with sardines,
cheese, onion, mayonnaise, seasoning
and parsley until smooth. Use to fill
inverted mushrooms. Garnish with
parsley sprigs.

Stuffed Celery

Cut celery stalks into 5 cm/2 inch pieces,
and fill with one of the following:

EGG AND ONION
Mix together chopped hard-boiled eggs,
mayonnaise, salt and pepper, and a
little finely chopped onion. Pipe on to
celery stalks and sprinkle with chopped
parsley.

ROQUEFORT
Mix together Roquefort or another blue
cheese with Worcestershire sauce,
mayonnaise, salt and pepper. Pipe on to
celery stalks and sprinkle with paprika.

VARIATION
Cut peeled cucumber into 2.5–5 cm/1–2
inch slices, and remove seeds with
an apple corer. Fill with one of the
above fillings.

Cheese Titbits

CHEESE DATES
Stone dates. Mix Roquefort or other blue cheese with butter until creamy, and pipe into dates. Spear on to cocktail sticks and arrange each date on a lettuce leaf.

CAMEMBERT SLICES
Top buttered bread rounds with Camembert wedges, and garnish with gherkin fans and fresh cress.

PUMPERNICKEL ROUNDS
Top buttered pumpernickel rounds with mixed pickles and strips of hard cheese. Add gherkins wrapped in cooked ham, and garnish with strips of pickled red pepper and parsley sprigs.

ANCHOVY ROUNDS
Spread rounds of pumpernickel with herb-flavoured cream cheese, add slices of tomato and hard-boiled egg, top with rolled anchovy fillets stuffed with lumpfish roe, and garnish with parsley.

STUFFED TOMATOES
Blend a soft cheese with cream and finely chopped pickled gherkin. Use to stuff hollowed-out tomato halves. Garnish with parsley, radish slices and paprika.

CHEESE BALLS
Beat cheese spread until smooth, then form into small balls. Toss in a mixture of pumpernickel crumbs and mild paprika, and spear on to savoury crackers.

SALMON ROLLS
Wrap pieces of Brie in slices of smoked salmon. Add a thin half slice of lemon and spear on to squares of buttered white bread.

CHEESE CUBES
Spear two stuffed olives on to a cube of hard cheese.

Spicy Beefballs

450 g/1 lb minced beef, raw
50 g/2 oz fresh white breadcrumbs
15 ml/1 tablespoon Worcestershire sauce
salt and pepper

Mix together all ingredients. Form into walnut-sized balls, then chill. Grill, turning frequently, or cook quickly in a frying pan with a little oil. Spear each ball with a cocktail stick, and serve hot, accompanied by Barbecue Sauce (p94).

Liver Sausage Rissolettes

100 g/4 oz plain flour
1.25 ml/¼ teaspoon salt
1 egg
250 ml/8 fl oz milk

FILLING
200 g/7 oz firm liver sausage
2.5 ml/½ teaspoon grated onion
salt and freshly ground black pepper
2 egg yolks
breadcrumbs
oil for deep frying

Sift flour and salt into a bowl, make a well in the centre and add egg. Stir in half the milk, and beat vigorously until mixture is smooth and bubbly. Stir in rest of milk. Use mixture to make pancakes about 7.5 cm/3 inches in diameter.

To make filling, mash sausage with onion, and season to taste. Roll each pancake round enough of mixture to enclose it completely. Tuck open ends under joined edge as for envelope flaps, then seal with egg yolk. Roll in yolk and breadcrumbs, and fry at 180°C/350°F, until crisped and brown on both sides. Drain thoroughly, then spear on to cocktail sticks, and serve at once.

Opposite: *Cheese Titbits*

Olives in Bacon

thin slices of streaky bacon, sliced
    in half
stuffed olives, drained
dried basil

GARNISH
lettuce leaves

Wrap a half slice of bacon round each
olive, and sprinkle with basil. Grill for
2 minutes on each side, then arrange on
lettuce leaves, and serve at once.

Prunes in Bacon

thin slices of streaky bacon, without
    rinds
juicy prunes

Roll a thin slice of bacon round each
prune, and fasten with a cocktail stick.
Fry in a frying pan until bacon is just
cooked and is golden-brown at edges.
Serve hot or cold.

Curried Sausages

cocktail sausages
curry powder

Roll cocktail sausages in curry powder to
give a fine even coating. Put on a baking
sheet, and cook at 180°C/350°F/Gas 4, for
about 20 minutes. Serve hot, speared on
to cocktail sticks.

Sprats Boursin

450 g/1 lb sprats
salt and black pepper
150 g/5 oz Boursin cheese
2 eggs, beaten
breadcrumbs
oil for deep frying

Clean and remove heads from sprats.
Remove backbone, then wash and dry.
Season to taste. Soften cheese, and use to
spread insides of sprats. Fold over to re-
form sprat shape. Dust in flour, dip in
beaten egg, coat in breadcrumbs and fry
at 180°C/350°F, for 4 minutes until crisp.
Drain, and serve hot.

Goujons of Plaice

plaice fillets
milk
seasoned flour
oil for deep frying

Cut fillets lengthways into short strips
about 2.5–5 cm/1–2 inches wide. Dip in
milk and coat with flour, then fry at
180°C/350°F, for 2–3 minutes until
golden-brown. Drain, and serve hot,
accompanied by Tartare Sauce (p94).

Smoked Salmon Rolls

cream cheese
horseradish, freshly grated
salt and freshly ground black
    pepper
strips of smoked salmon, thinly
    sliced

Season cream cheese with horseradish,
salt and pepper, then spread on to slices
of salmon. Roll up into cigarette shapes,
and secure with cocktail sticks.

Buttered Savoury Almonds

225 g/8 oz blanched almonds
50 g/2 oz butter
10 ml/2 teaspoons olive **or** corn oil
2.5 ml/½ teaspoon salt
5 ml/1 teaspoon paprika

Fry almonds gently in butter and oil for
3–4 minutes, or until a pale golden, turning often. Remove from pan, drain, and
sprinkle with salt mixed with paprika.
Serve hot or cold.

Devilled Brazils

225 g/8 oz Brazil nuts
50 g/2 oz butter
10 ml/2 teaspoons olive **or** corn oil
5 ml/1 teaspoon each dry mustard
    and paprika
5 ml/1 teaspoon each celery and
    onion salt
shake each of Cayenne pepper and
    garlic salt

Slice nuts fairly thickly. Fry gently in
butter and oil for 3–4 minutes, or until a
pale golden, turning often. Remove from
pan, drain, and sprinkle with seasonings.
Serve hot or cold.

Dips

Camembert Cream

75 g/3 oz butter, softened
200 g/7 oz Camembert cheese
    (not over-ripe)
5 ml/1 teaspoon mild paprika
1 small onion, diced
small bunch of chives, chopped

GARNISH
pretzels
savoury stick biscuits
1 pumpernickel cocktail round
1 radish water lily

Cream butter until soft and white. Mash Camembert with fork and mix with butter. Add paprika, and mix well together. Stir in onion and chives. Arrange on a plate, and garnish with pretzels, savoury stick biscuits, the pumpernickel and a radish water lily.

Camembert Cream

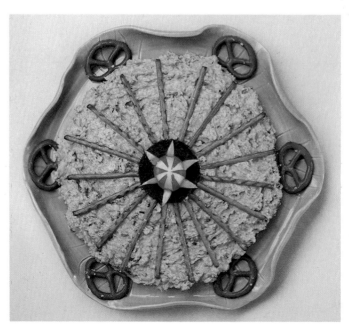

Cream Cheese Dip

250 g/9 oz cream cheese
45 ml/3 tablespoons mayonnaise
30 ml/2 tablespoons soured cream
salt and pepper
10 ml/2 teaspoons paprika
10 ml/2 teaspoons curry powder
sprigs of parsley, finely chopped
sprigs of fresh dill, finely chopped
chives, finely chopped
cress, finely chopped

Sieve cream cheese, then mix to a smooth sauce with mayonnaise and soured cream. Season to taste and divide into three portions. Season one portion with paprika, the second with curry powder and the third with parsley, dill, chives and cress.

Serve with chicory leaves, small crackers, savoury stick biscuits and strips of pickled cucumber.

Party Egg Ball

75 g/3 oz cream cheese
75 g/3 oz Cheddar cheese, grated
4 hard-boiled eggs, finely chopped
6 stuffed olives, chopped
125 g/5 oz canned shrimps, drained
4 gherkins, finely chopped
1 green pepper, deseeded and
  chopped
salt and pepper
15 ml/1 tablespoon sherry
75 g/3 oz walnuts, chopped

Beat cream cheese until smooth, then add Cheddar cheese, and mix well. Add eggs and all other ingredients apart from walnuts. Mix well together, shape into a ball, wrap in foil and chill for 1 hour. Toss cheese ball in walnuts in a polythene bag until well coated. Serve on a flat plate, accompanied by savoury crackers.

Cottage Cabbage Dip

1 small cabbage
225 g/8 oz cottage cheese
175 g/6 oz Stilton cheese
½ small cucumber, diced
3 hard-boiled eggs, chopped
142 ml/5 fl oz carton soured cream
1.25 ml/¼ teaspoon nutmeg
salt and pepper

GARNISH
paprika

Carefully remove cabbage heart, keeping outer leaves intact to serve as the serving dish. Mix all ingredients together and pile into cabbage shell. Chill, then sprinkle with paprika.

Serve with savoury biscuits, crisps or raw vegetables.

Party Egg Ball, Cottage Cabbage Dip

Beetroot Dip

225 g/8 oz cottage cheese
30 ml/2 tablespoons mayonnaise
150 g/5 oz carton natural yoghurt **or**
   142 ml/5 fl oz carton soured cream
2 small beetroot, grated

Sieve cottage cheese into a bowl. Stir in mayonnaise and yoghurt or soured cream. Just before serving, stir in beetroot.

Serve with sticks of vegetables, savoury crackers or crisps.

Celery Dip

225 g/8 oz Danish blue cheese
10 ml/2 teaspoons onion, grated
2 sticks celery, finely chopped
60 ml/4 tablespoons milk
celery leaves

Mash cheese with fork until smooth, then add remaining ingredients, mixing well until fairly soft. Add more milk, if necessary. Serve in a bowl, garnished with celery leaves.

Serve with cauliflower florets, sticks of carrot or potato crisps.

Paprika Dip

200 g/7 oz quark **or** curd cheese
60 ml/4 tablespoons evaporated
   milk
10 ml/2 teaspoons paprika
2 small onions, finely chopped
2 pickled gherkins, chopped
salt
garlic powder
pinch of grated nutmeg

Beat together cheese and evaporated milk until smooth. Add paprika and continue beating until mixture is an even pink colour throughout. Mix onions and gherkins with cheese, and season to taste with salt, garlic powder and nutmeg.

Serve with savoury biscuits or raw vegetable sticks.

Avocado Dip

2 avocadoes, peeled and stoned
175 g/6 oz cream cheese
120 ml/8 tablespoons single cream
20–30 ml/4–6 teaspoons vinegar
salt and pepper
2 cloves garlic, crushed

Mash avocadoes until smooth, then add cream cheese, cream and vinegar. Mix well together. Season to taste with salt, pepper and garlic. Turn dip into avocado shells or a bowl, and surround with fingers of crisp vegetables such as carrots, celery, spring onion and radishes.

Blue Cheese Dip

50 g/2 oz Stilton
100 g/4 oz cottage cheese
30 ml/2 tablespoons chives, finely
   chopped
150 ml/¼ pint single cream
salt and pepper

Mash Stilton with a fork until smooth, then mix in cottage cheese, chives and cream. Season to taste, then serve in a bowl surrounded by assorted crisp biscuits.

Blue Cheese Dunk

225 g/8 oz cream cheese
100 g/4 oz blue cheese
2 eggs, beaten
30 ml/2 tablespoons mayonnaise
10 ml/2 teaspoons lemon juice
1.25 ml/¼ teaspoon garlic salt
2.5 ml/½ teaspoon dried basil

Beat cream cheese until smooth, then crumble in blue cheese. Gradually beat in eggs, then add remaining ingredients, and mix well.

Serve with crisps, savoury biscuits or raw vegetables.

Cheese and Olive Dip

225 g/8 oz cream cheese
10 ml/2 teaspoons concentrated
 tomato purée
15 ml/1 tablespoon Worcestershire
 sauce
1.25 ml/¼ teaspoon lemon juice
25 g/1 oz gherkins, chopped
25 g/1 oz stuffed olives, chopped
salt and pepper

Blend together cream cheese, tomato purée, Worcestershire sauce and lemon juice. Fold in gherkins and olives, and chill until required.

Serve with biscuits, crisps, Melba toast, sticks of carrots or celery, fingers of pepper, cauliflower florets or button mushrooms.
Note If dip is too thick, thin down with a little single cream.

Pâté Dip

100 g/4 oz liver sausage
75 g/3 oz cream cheese
15 ml/1 tablespoon Worcestershire
 sauce
75 ml/5 tablespoons single cream
salt and pepper

Mash liver sausage with cream cheese and Worcestershire sauce. Stir in cream to give a softer consistency. Season to taste and turn into a bowl. Surround with small pieces of Melba toast.

Derby Dip

225 g/8 oz cottage cheese
100 g/4 oz Sage Derby cheese,
 grated
5 radishes
150 g/5 oz carton natural yoghurt

Sieve cottage cheese into a bowl. Stir in 75 g/3 oz of Sage Derby. Chop four of the radishes and stir in with yoghurt. Spoon into a dish. Garnish with remaining cheese and radish.

Serve with crisps, savoury crackers or sticks of celery, carrot or cauliflower florets.

Horseradish Dip with Cheese

125 g/5 oz quark **or** curd cheese
60 ml/4 tablespoons single cream
22.5 ml/1½ tablespoons
    horseradish, freshly grated
salt
sugar
2.5 ml/½ teaspoon paprika

Beat cheese until soft, and mix together with cream and horseradish. Season to taste with salt, sugar and paprika.
    Serve with savoury crackers, crisps or sticks of fresh vegetables.

Horseradish Dip with Apples and Nuts

4 apples, peeled, halved and cored
juice of 1 lemon
90 ml/6 tablespoons mayonnaise
30 ml/2 tablespoons
    horseradish, freshly grated
60 ml/4 tablespoons ground
    hazelnuts

Grate apples finely, then mix immediately with lemon juice. Blend together mayonnaise and horseradish, add hazelnuts, and mix together with grated apples.
    Serve with savoury crackers, crisps or sticks of fresh vegetables.

Horseradish Dip with Ham

45 ml/3 tablespoons mayonnaise
15 ml/1 tablespoon
    horseradish, freshly grated
salt and pepper
dash of Tabasco sauce
75 g/3 oz cooked ham, diced
1 small pickled cucumber, diced

Mix together mayonnaise and horseradish, and season to taste with salt, pepper and Tabasco sauce. Mix in diced ham and cucumber.
    Serve with savoury crackers, crisps or sticks of fresh vegetables.

Horseradish Dip with Cheese,
Horseradish Dip with Apples and Nuts,
Horseradish Dip with Ham

Mustard Dip

2 apples, peeled, halved and cored
45 ml/3 tablespoons lemon juice
2 hard-boiled egg yolks
120 ml/8 tablespoons soured cream
45 ml/3 tablespoons hot made
    mustard
salt and pepper
pinch of sugar

Grate apples, then mix immediately with lemon juice. Sieve yolks into apples, mix in soured cream and mustard, and stir until smooth. Season well with salt, pepper and sugar. Cover and chill for 20 minutes before serving.
  Serve with savoury biscuits, crisps or raw vegetables.

Sweet Pickle Dip

120 ml/8 tablespoons double cream
120 ml/8 tablespoons mayonnaise
90 ml/6 tablespoons sweet pickle
salt and pepper

Whip cream until stiff and combine with mayonnaise and pickle. Season to taste.
  Serve with raw button mushrooms and cubes of hard cheese.

Onion and Egg Dip

2 hard-boiled eggs, finely chopped
142 ml/5/fl oz carton soured cream
½ pkt onion soup mix

GARNISH
paprika

Mix together all ingredients, and sprinkle with paprika.
  Serve with crisps.

Crab Dip

150 ml/¼ pint soured cream
25 g/1 oz onion, finely chopped
15 ml/1 tablespoon crabmeat

Mix together all the ingredients, then chill for 2–3 hours to allow the flavours to develop.
  Serve with cubed apples, cauliflower florets, strips of pepper or carrot, or with potato crisps.

Egg and Avocado Dip

4 avocadoes, peeled and stoned
6 hard-boiled eggs, chopped
4 tomatoes, skinned, deseeded and
    chopped
60 ml/4 tablespoons lemon juice
60 ml/4 tablespoons mayonnaise

GARNISH
paprika
chopped parsley

Dice avocadoes, and mix with all ingredients, then blend for 20 seconds in an electric blender. Serve in avocado shells, sprinkled with paprika and chopped parsley.
  Serve with savoury biscuits, crisps or raw vegetables.

Smoked Mackerel Dip

4 whole hot smoked mackerel,
    skinned and boned **or** 4 single
    fillets
100 g/4 oz butter, softened
2 cloves garlic, crushed (optional)
90 ml/6 tablespoons mayonnaise
30 ml/2 tablespoons horseradish
    sauce
30 ml/2 tablespoons lemon juice
salt and freshly ground black
    pepper

Flake fish, add butter and garlic, and pound well. Mix together with mayonnaise and horseradish sauce, then stir in lemon juice and seasoning to taste.
  Serve with strips of red and green pepper, cucumber, celery, cauliflower florets and small savoury biscuits.

Cocktail Dip for Prawns

200 g/7 oz tomato ketchup
15 ml/1 tablespoon lemon juice
10 ml/2 teaspoons horseradish,
    freshly grated
2.5 ml/½ teaspoon salt
pinch of sugar
small pinch of Cayenne pepper
pinch of garlic powder

GARNISH
prawns
lettuce leaves

Mix together all ingredients. Spear prawns on to cocktail sticks and arrange on lettuce leaves. Use to dip into sauce.

Barbecue Sauce

30 ml/2 tablespoons cooking oil
2 onions, grated
850 g/30 oz canned peeled tomatoes
75 ml/5 tablespoons Worcestershire
    sauce
20 ml/4 teaspoons cornflour
30 ml/2 tablespoons water
5 ml/1 teaspoon salt
15 ml/1 tablespoon sugar

Heat oil in pan and cook gently for 3 minutes. Add onions, tomatoes and Worcestershire sauce. Cover and simmer for 15 minutes, stirring from time to time. Sieve or liquidize. Blend cornflour with water, stir into sauce and bring to boil, stirring all the time. Season to taste with salt and sugar.
    Serve with Spicy Beefballs (p84).

Tartare Sauce

10 ml/2 teaspoons gherkins,
    chopped
10 ml/2 teaspoons olives, chopped
10 ml/2 teaspoons capers, chopped
10 ml/2 teaspoons parsley, chopped
10 ml/2 teaspoons chives, chopped
300 ml/½ pint mayonnaise
2.5 ml/½ teaspoon French mustard
20 ml/4 teaspoons wine vinegar **or**
    lemon juice

Fold chopped ingredients into mayonnaise with mustard, then add vinegar or lemon juice. Leave to stand for at least 1 hour before serving for flavours to blend.
    Serve with Goujons of Plaice (p87).

Index of Cocktails

Index of Snacks